Chickens & Pigs

Chickens & Pigs

Business Models and
Competitive Strategy

HAROLD STAR

Emba Press
P. O. Box 303
Getzville, New York 14068-0303
www.embapress.com

ISBN: 978-0-9646962-0-4 (PB)

Library of Congress Control Number: 2007932308

Contents

Figures

Tables

Preface

Without our acquisition of a stake in Volkswagen, the risk (for our business model) would have threatened our very existence." (Wendelin Wiedeking, CEO, Porsche, cited by Richard Milne in "Wiedeking Breaks Silence on Long-term Strategy." *Financial Times,* December 8, 2005, 31.)

Wiedeking's words sound ominous. Porsche's *business model* was at risk, and the company's existence was in jeopardy. As a defense of Porsche's business model, Wiedeking's investment in Volkswagen secured the company's long-term future.

Wiedeking's words are compelling, his argument powerful. But what does he mean when he refers to the company's "business model"?

Business models are undeniably strategic, but in what sense? Do they influence strategies, as Wiedeking implies? Are they separate from an organization's strategy, or are they a part of that strategy? Are business models the means of implementing a strategy? Or is it the reverse: do strategies implement business models?

The term "business model" is widely accepted in the business world and popular press. The dot.com era provided a stream of companies in search of a business model, companies constantly revamping their business model, and companies failing—sometimes spectacularly—for lack of a business model. The end of the dot.com era, coinciding with the record-breaking NASDAQ slide of late 2001, did not bring an end to the popular currency of the term. As shown below, the term is now firmly ensconced in the mainstream.

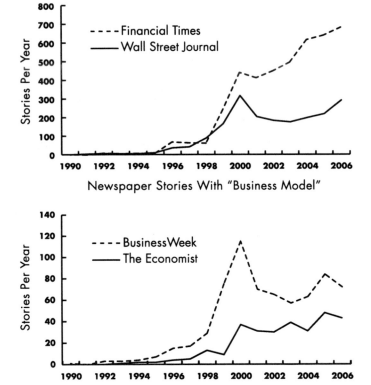

FIGURE P.1 APPEARANCES OF "BUSINESS MODEL" IN THE POPULAR PRESS

Virtually all these articles use the term "business model" in the same way that Wiedeking does, without defining it. Supreme Court Justice

Potter Stewart once said of pornography that he couldn't define it but could recognize it when he saw it. This seems to be the status of business models: easy to identify, hard to define.

The academic in me is uncomfortable with this. I've spent my professional life attempting to inculcate in others the logical thinking and careful analysis required in order to understand how businesses work. This book is my attempt to bring some logic and definition to how business models are created and used. Specifically, I want to answer two questions: What are business models? What roles do they play in an organization's strategies? *I believe that business models are the root of everything strategic.*

But this is not an academic book. I'm a full-time academic who was once a full-time CEO. I still run a small consulting practice. While this book describes strategy as I've learned it and used it in real-world situations, its content has been analyzed and tested by my academic nature.

If you're a *strategist*—that is, if you're an executive with market-level responsibility for the performance of a company or a division—this book will open your eyes to a new way of seeing your business, revealing the source of your company's strategic challenges and enabling you to understand what you need to do to meet them.

If you're *involved with mergers and acquisitions,* whether as a direct participant or an advisor, this book will give you the means to assess the long-term viability of a business. You'll learn new metrics that apply to both due diligence and company valuation.

If you're a *marketer* whose customers are other businesses, you'll find that an understanding of business models as I've defined them will free you from the constraints of a needs-based, consumer marketing perspective. This book's point of view can be the source of powerful, effective marketing campaigns that will benefit your company and your customers.

Understanding—*really understanding*—business models will give you a new way to see and comprehend businesses. This book not only explains the nature of this new view of business models, it also translates this deeper understanding into logical and practical insights that high-level executives can use to create and manage their own business models.

Now, if you're wondering what on earth chickens and pigs have to do with business models, read on.

Harold Star
Buffalo, New York
March 2006

Acknowledgements

This book has been more than 12 years in the making, and many people have helped along the way. My deepest thanks go to Michael Bryant, Charles Walton, John Stephan, Stephen Snyder, and Jerry Bierman. Without their input, I would have been unable to articulate, develop, or extend the framework that follows.

My wife, Shirley, never realized that by marrying me she became my primary editor. She worked on each of this book's many versions, even though it got to the point that her eyes would glaze when I brought her one more "final" draft. She was always ready to help, and I can't begin to thank her for the patience and diligence she has shown in fulfilling this role.

Of the many others who contributed to this project, some brought ideas, some brought hard work, some brought both. I hesitate to name them individually because I fear I might omit someone unintentionally. Instead, I thank you all collectively.

One group deserves special gratitude. Since February 2002, my students have been captive guinea pigs to many of these arguments, subjected to different explanations of the framework described in this book. Many contributed ideas that appear in these pages; even more shared firsthand stories of how practices and experiences of their organizations matched concepts I was presenting. To my executive and professional MBA classes, my undergraduate students, and the executives who attended my Center for Entrepreneurial Leadership strategy classes, thank you. You taught me more than I taught you.

Finally, I must acknowledge the enduring contributions of two of my former professors. Ron Crawford, my mentor, taught me how to think. Henry Mintzberg gave me permission to do so in pictures. I'm honored to say every page that follows bears their influence.

Introduction

This book is about strategic management. You may already know some or most of the terms you're about to encounter, but to make sure we're on the same page, this introduction provides a brief overview of the strategic management discipline.

STRATEGIC MANAGEMENT

In the business world, strategic management goes by many names. You may call the field "strategic planning," "policy," or "business policy." You may have studied the topic in college or university in a course known as "Policy and Strategy." Today, all these terms refer to "strategic management."

The academic world began calling the field "strategic management" in the late 1970s, when the discipline emerged as a unique domain of theory and research. But strategic management means more than management of a company's strategy; it further conveys that *all* management practices should be infused with the company's overall strategy. Thus, strategic management has meaning for both executives and lower-level management.

For executive-level management, the term "strategic management" means managing the overall strategy of the business—what we can call "organizational strategy." Strategic decisions at this level typically have a whole-enterprise, long-term orientation. In theory, to be a strategist is to be somewhat above day-to-day events and internal squabbles.

For managers within the business itself (generally called "functional managers"), strategic management's central dictate is that they should make their units' objectives consistent with the organization's strategy. "Strategic marketing" and "strategic human resources" are examples of disciplines that have developed branches with the specific purpose of incorporating organizational strategy into their practices.

A core assumption of strategic management is that, within a business, strategy comes first. All parts of the business must support the strategy, with each part making its contribution to pursuit of the strategic goal. Strategy thus imparts order and coherence to a company's internal and external behaviors.

INTELLECTUAL ROOTS

Economics dominates the way strategists see the world today. When you encounter an author or analyst who speaks of "industry," "competitive advantage," or "value," you should recognize that these are concepts that have come from one the many branches of economics.

Economics is not the only intellectual stream from which strategists have drawn ideas, however. The social science disciplines of sociology and social psychology have both contributed to the strategy realm. When you encounter terms like "organizations," "environments," "decision making," and "uncertainty," you should recognize these as topics rooted in the social sciences.

Core assumptions of these root disciplines vary widely. Economists, for example, see the world as more rational and less conflict-laden than do sociologists. Economists see economic motivations driving individual behaviors, while psychologists see a whole complex of alternative motivators. Sociologists see power and conflict as characteristics of organizations, while psychologists see need and motivation. Economists see groups of self-interested companies, while sociologists see networks of organizations characterized by relationships that can be either competitive or cooperative.

These assumptions, and the analyses and prescriptions they generate, tend to cluster together into coherent, self-contained views of business and the range of organizational strategies that can—and should—be pursued. We call these viewpoints *paradigms*.

PARADIGMS

Academics use the term "paradigm" to describe a "prevailing view"—i.e., the totality of assumptions, concepts, and practices accepted by those who study a field of activity. In his landmark volume, *The Structure of Scientific Revolutions,* Thomas Kuhn describes the evolution of science as a process in which one paradigm replaces another.

While strategic management is a relatively young discipline, three distinct phases and two separate paradigms can be identified within it. In the 1970s and early 1980s, strategic management had not yet coalesced around a single paradigm. McGill University's Henry Mintzberg, one of the most active theorists and writers in this phase of the discipline, at one point identified as many as eleven "schools of strategic thought," each with its own unique perspective.

By the mid-1980s, the viewpoint of Harvard University's Michael Porter had taken hold. The model he brought to strategic management was adapted from a branch of economics called "industrial organization." Porter taught that industries are composed of five elements or "forces." He showed managers how to learn the structure of their industries and how to develop "generic" strategies to cope with the prevailing forces. His overall approach was so robust that both academics and business executives found merit in the view.

While researchers found that Porter's ideas were generally valid, cracks soon appeared in their ranks. Debate erupted over how much of a role industry played in a company's success or failure. Some began to question the extent of separation between the generic strategies. Still others found the five-forces framework to be better suited to the slow-moving world of the 1950s rather than the modern world of globalization and technology-driven change that was beginning to emerge in the 1980s.

By the mid-1990s, a different view of the strategic management landscape emerged. The new, resource-based view (RBV) incorporated aspects of the old paradigm (external analysis) while offering a differing perspective (internal, company-specific aspects) on what made one company more profitable than another.

RBV theorists point to *resource types* (such as capabilities, knowledge, and processes) and *resource characteristics* (such as inimitability and substitutability) as factors related to relative levels of profitability. Where Porter saw strategy as a matter of establishing a position within a turbulent competitive space, proponents of the RBV see instead the need to build, and wield, strategic resources.

The RBV is today dominant within academic circles, with scholarly research efforts probing at the many facets and implications of the perspective.

THE "STRATEGY" IN STRATEGIC MANAGEMENT

In the years when strategic management was emerging as a discipline, the nature of "strategy" was debated, often fiercely. Henry Mintzberg observed that different analysts saw strategy in four different ways:

1. Some saw strategy as a *plan*—i.e., a deliberate, often formalized, statement of the intent and the means to achieve the desired end.

2. Others saw strategy as a *position* to be established and occupied within a company's competitive space.

3. To others, strategy was a matter of *perception*—i.e., a way of seeing the world.

4. Mintzberg himself saw strategy as a *pattern* within decisions and actions.

Although Mintzberg's observations date back more than 20 years, they remain valid today. It's easy to find authors or analysts, for example, who advocate that strategists should develop a "vision," formalize an organizational "mission," or define their companies' objectives with an ambitious statement of "intent." Such themes and concepts are examples of strategy as perception.

"Strategy as position" dominated strategic management through the 1980s. Porter's descriptions of industry structure and generic strategies effectively described competitive "landscapes" and the positions a company could "stake out" on them. This perspective remains a centerpiece of virtually every contemporary strategy textbook.

When the RBV emerged as a paradigm to replace Porter's viewpoint, terms like "competitive advantage," "resources," "core competencies," and "capabilities" became common. To create strategic resources, contemporary managers typically strive to "align" internal activities and refine organizational processes. Though not quite how

Mintzberg saw the idea in the 1970s, these efforts are reflective of strategy as a pattern.

Most executives think of strategizing as developing a written plan. Often they see the ideal plan as brief, simple, action-oriented, and with measurable goals. I've worked with executives who like to see their company's strategic plan reduced to a checklist that can be kept at hand, with to-do items waiting to be scratched off. I've worked with others who believe the only way to implement a strategy is to reduce everything down to a set of metrics that can be regularly reviewed because, in their words, "What gets measured gets done."

Many academics, in contrast, see strategies as more complex than a list that will fit on a sheet of paper. They don't see strategies as "planned" but instead see strategies as formed, crafted, and often created unintentionally (sometimes by accident or error). Mainline strategy texts never describe strategy as a plan.

LEVELS OF STRATEGY

Strategic management typically distinguishes between "business-level" strategy and "corporate-level" strategy.

Business-level strategy concerns itself with matters like attracting customers, fending off rivals, and establishing sustainable positions within industry environments. Business-level strategy is synonymous with competitive strategy.

Corporate-level strategy is concerned with creating and managing a multi-business entity. Related topics include mergers and acquisitions, vertical integration, diversification, and organizational structure. Corporate strategists struggle with imprecise concepts like "fit" and "relatedness" to assess and manage the relationship between

- the corporate whole and its constituent parts,

- individual parts of the corporate whole, and
- a contemplated acquisition and the acquiring company.

The long-standing holy grail of corporate strategy is creation of a multi-business enterprise that is *synergistic*, one that is worth more than the sum of its parts. To find synergy, strategists typically look for "strategic fit" between the different businesses within the corporation. Theorists have long held that fit is most likely when the businesses within the corporation are "related" to each other.

The criteria that measure "relatedness" have been debated extensively, and assessing strategic fit is often more art than science. Therefore, the quest for synergy has been largely unsuccessful. In many business combinations, anticipated synergies didn't materialize; in other cases, the generated synergies weren't enough to recover the excessively high price paid to bring the units together. In more than a few cases, synergy was little more than false justification for a business combination that was otherwise without merit or logic.

Most strategists today view *competitive advantage* as a necessary, but not sufficient, condition of market success. The concept has become so widespread that academic treatments now often define business strategy as the pursuit of competitive advantage. *Corporate advantage*, a variant, has become widely used as a corporate strategy tool.

The pursuit and attainment of competitive advantage is said by scholars to involve both external and internal analysis. External analysis is a formal assessment of the characteristics of the business's industry and broader environments—a process meant to identify what a company "should" do. If you're familiar with SWOT analysis (Strengths, Weaknesses, Opportunities, Threats), external analysis is the identification and analysis of the company's opportunities and threats. Terms like "five forces," "strategic groups," and "environment" are commonly used for external analysis.

Internal analysis, in contrast, involves analysis of resources a company already possesses—resources SWOT would identify as the company's strengths and weaknesses. Internal analysis strives to determine what a company "can" do to take advantage of opportunities and either mitigate or avoid threats. Contemporary academic strategists regard key internal resources, also called "strategic resources," as the cornerstone of competitive advantage. They see internal factors as critical to external success. Terms like "core competencies," "value chain," and "culture" are elements of internal analysis associated with competitive advantage. So, too, are concepts like "knowledge" and "processes."

WHO DEVELOPS STRATEGY?

Theoretically, executive-level management develops and articulates an organization's strategy. And, theoretically, an organization's strategy emerges from a formal process. Finally, and once again theoretically, the principal strategist is the chief executive officer, the CEO. In practice, strategy formulation is actually much messier.

Strategic management has long distinguished strategy *formulation* from strategy *implementation*. Formulation is cognitive, the development of management's intention to move the organization in a certain direction or along a particular path. Formulation is always regarded as the responsibility of executive-level management.

Implementation, on the other hand, is the matter of translating executive-level management intentions into organizational actions and thus is the domain of all organization members. As anybody who has managed or coached knows, the gap between the leader's intent and the implemented actions can be wide. Military strategists know this gap better than most; their carefully articulated battle plans are often tossed aside when the enemy is engaged and individual soldiers have to make real-time decisions with life-or-death consequences. These strategists describe the gap between their intentions and their soldiers' actions on the battlefield as "the fog of war."

Modern business executives must deal with their own variant of the fog of war. Consider, for example, the fact that organizational representatives working with a customer are often confronted with requests requiring yes or no decisions. Customers today don't want to wait for a representative to check with the head office on whether or not the request is approved, a process that can take days, weeks, or even months. They want the answer immediately.

If the company representative wants to avoid losing the customer to a rival, he or she must make immediate decisions based upon his or her own best assessments of (a) what the executive team is trying to achieve and (b) which answer to the customer request will most effectively further the organization's best interests. In making such decisions, the field representative can be right, but he or she can just as easily be wrong.

Such gaps between management intentions and implemented actions within an organization can occur in other parts of the business. Internally, they can arise when employees have the opportunity to make decisions that involve trade-offs between efficiency and effectiveness. They can similarly arise when employees have the opportunity to choose between what is known (i.e., the proven and well-established ways) and the unknown (i.e., new, untried options). In general, the gap between the executive team's intention and any implemented action is a function of

- the *size* of the organization (the greater the number of employees, the wider the gap is likely to be) and/or
- the *complexity* of the organization (the fewer the layers of management, the wider the gap will be) and/or
- the *geographic dispersion* of the organization (the broader the geographic scope of the business, the wider the gap will likely be).

And to complicate things a little more, keep in mind that the gap between management's intention and the organization's implemented action isn't always dysfunctional. Returning to the example noted above, the representative in the field is closer to the customer than the executive who designed the strategy. Decisions made by field operatives may positively adapt management's strategy, thereby making it more effective. Yes, strategy development is messy.

BUSINESS MODELS & STRATEGIC MANAGEMENT

It's fair to say the academic world has largely ignored the business model concept. The top-level academic journals have not once published either a conceptual or empirical article reviewing the concept. The only mainline journal in which the term even occasionally crops up is *Harvard Business Review*.

In general, when strategy scholars have written about the subject, they've struggled to define the boundary between strategy and models. Joan Magretta described a business model as a story that explains how enterprises work. The story, she argued, is wide ranging, touching everything from defining the customer to how the business makes money. Regarding strategy, she says that a business model isn't the same thing as a strategy. . . . Business models describe, as a system, how the pieces of a business fit together. But they don't factor in one critical dimension of performance: competition. Sooner or later—and it is usually sooner—every enterprise runs into competitors. Dealing with that reality is strategy's job. ("Why business models matter." *Harvard Business Review,* May 2002, 91.)

Magretta implies that what is competitive is inherently strategic and, by extension, what isn't competitive is therefore part of the business model. This is a position that would make many academics uncomfortable. Donald Hambrick and James Fredrickson, for example, clearly incorporate what Magretta would call "story elements" into their definition of strategy.

George Yip is another academic writer who incorporates strategy concepts into his definition of a business model. Whereas Magretta used competition as the basis for distinguishing between strategic issues and model-related issues, Yip sees strategy as the means by which business models are implemented and then changed when necessary.

If any of this confuses you, I've made my point. Academics in general haven't turned their attention to the concept of business models, and those few who have written on the subject haven't reached consensus on its attributes or relationships to other strategic variables.

CONCLUSION

An essential aspect of defining anything is making clear what that thing is *not*. In general, the framework I call "Chickens & Pigs" (C&P) diverges from the norm in important ways.

First and foremost, C&P begins with a completely new approach to business models: what they are, where they come from, and their impact upon strategy.

In some cases this new approach forced me to create new concepts (the customer pool, for example); in other cases, C&P forced me to modify the way I approached existing concepts. Some of these modifications involved taking liberties. In fact, C&P essentially redefines what Peter Drucker called the "theory of the firm."

Some readers will find that C&P provokes considerable dissonance, representing as it does a departure from the well-established territory described in this chapter. Others may experience no dissonance at all.

Whatever your reaction, please keep in mind that C&P is intended to be a complement to the main body of strategic management knowledge. I'm not asking you to abandon old ideas and perspectives. I'm simply offering you a different way to view your world.

1

Business Models

Put yourself into the role of consultant to the CEO of Boots and Coots (AMEX: WEL). What advice would you give Jerry Winchester, company CEO?

BOOTS AND COOTS

Boots and Coots is one of the few companies that fight oil-well fires. The company's service is technically complex and requires highly specialized resources. Customers are more than willing to pay a premium price for the company's help and call upon Boots and Coots because of its well-earned reputation.

The company's "modern period" began in the middle of 1997 when the managers of International Well Control (IWC) took over Boots and Coots. By the end of 1998, the newly constituted Boots and Coots had completed five "complementary" acquisitions. Elements from these acquisitions were clearly part of the company's three major businesses described in the company's 2002 10K filing:

1. *Prevention.* Boots and Coots provided clients inspections, training, and preparedness planning. The company also operated Safe-

guard, a program through which Boots and Coots sold fire fighting equipment to oil producers and then maintained the preparedness of these "fire stations" by maintaining the equipment and conducting on-site safety inspections and emergency response drills.

2. *Response.* While the bulk of this company's revenues were associated with "critical events" (events in which hydrocarbons are either burning or escaping), they also earned revenue from "noncritical" events (subsurface operating problems) and from the rental of specialty equipment used for fire fighting and well control.

3. *Restoration.* Boots and Coots offered a variety of containment and reclamation services for oil and other hazardous materials spills.

The company's finances were not nearly as strong as the resources it had assembled. As shown in Table 1.1, the years 1997 through 2002 were unprofitable. Creditors were constantly being held at bay, sometimes barely, and the company was in danger of being delisted from the American Stock Exchange.

TABLE 1.1   BOOTS AND COOTS' FINANCES

YEAR (DECEMBER)	REVENUE ($ MILLION)	NET INCOME ($ MILLION)	NET PROFIT MARGIN (%)	EMPLOYEES
2003	35.9	7.1	19.8	39
2002	14.1	(9.2)		46
2001	36.1	1.2	3.3	173
2000	23.5	(21.3)		196
1999	67.6	(31.1)		354
1998	76.3	(3.0)		602
1997	5.4	(0.8)		25

Source: www.hoovers.com

Winchester became CEO in 2002, when company finances were at their most precarious. Facing a major liquidity crisis, he led a company-wide reorganization. The Restoration business was dropped, and many of the units acquired in the 1997–1998 period were divested.

As shown in Table 1.2, 2003 ended well. Both the Prevention and Response businesses enjoyed demand and profit surges.

A major part of the company's 2003 turnaround was the war in Iraq. As a subcontractor for Halliburton (NYSE: HAL), Boots and Coots participated in the Restore Iraqi Oil (RIO) program. Roughly three-quarters of that year's Response revenues were directly attributable to RIO-related work. At the beginning of 2004, that contract was renewed for a two-year period.

TABLE 1.2 PERFORMANCE OF BOOTS AND COOTS' BUSINESS SEGMENTS

	2000	2001	2002	2003
Revenues				
Prevention	1,564	5,189	7,666	16,159
Response	9,249	11,749	6,436	19,776
Total	10,813	16,938	14,102	35,935
Operating Income				
Prevention	-858	913	-732	3,731
Response	-2,505	3,494	-807	6,503
Total	-3,363	4,407	-1,539	10,234

(All figures $,000)

With Prevention revenues expected to grow 35 to 45 percent, Winchester predicted 2004 would be a very good year, independent of Iraq-based activities:

Absent Iraq, with the contribution from our other Response revenues in the first quarter and the Prevention revenues expected over the next three quarters, this company is at a point of being self sustained, and any additional Response revenues will have a direct positive impact on cash flow and earnings. (2003 Year-end Earnings Call, http://www.bootsandcoots.com/investor/2004_conference–call.htm, March 25, 2004.)

Imagine it's the middle of 2004 and Winchester is preparing for a meeting with the company's creditors. He asks you two strategic questions:

1. Considering its unsurpassed range of capabilities and proven track record, why has Boots and Coots been so unstable since its inception?
2. Has eliminating the Restoration business and retaining the Prevention business "fixed" Boots and Coots? Were these sound strategic moves? If so, why?

ANALYSIS

To understand Boots and Coots' problems, we must examine each of the company's businesses. The core business, its legacy unit, is the Response business. This is the business the company first established, and it was the foundation of the company they extended when they bought IWC.

The Response business suffers chronic cash flow problems. Ironically mirroring a characteristic of its customers, Response is a boom-and-bust business. In one period, the unit may be awash in cash; in the next period, cash flow may dry up completely.

To make matters worse, cash flows are inherently unpredictable. Response is driven by client accidents. While it may be possible to draw connections between overall economic activity and the likelihood of accidents, or to draw links between the likelihood of accidents and the price of oil, such connections are so flimsy they would be of interest only to academics and/or policy makers. Boots and Coots executives would be hard pressed to find value in such exercises, let alone use them as a basis for strategic decision making.

Fueled as it is by client crises, Boots and Coots can do nothing to drum up business during slow periods. The company is already known to potential clients, so there is little to be gained by aggressive marketing. Boots and Coots' Response business must wait for clients to come to them.

Then there is the other side of Boots and Coots' Response business: when it has work, cash gushes in. The process of extinguishing a well fire, and doing so quickly, is complex and challenging. Every job is unique, and every job demands a customized solution. The Response business can command whatever price Boots and Coots feels it needs to charge; the price of a Response solution is a function of both client urgency and the scale of the client's problem. The Response business has the potential to generate prodigious revenues. Boots and Coots can generate millions of dollars from a single Response contract.

Prevention is a very different business from Response. Whereas the Response business resolves a client's critical and immediate problem, Prevention is oriented toward managing an ongoing accident prevention process, rather than offering a clear and finite resolution to a client's problem. Response is a *project* business while Prevention is a *program* business.

Prevention doesn't enjoy the pricing freedom of the Response business. Before clients engage the services of the Prevention business, they almost assuredly conduct a cost/benefit analysis to measure how much their exposure to accidents would be reduced by Boots and Coots' Prevention services. The general nature of the Prevention business's service means it's likely Boots and Coots has direct rivals in this business area. The existence of these rivals further limits the price Boots and Coots might charge for Prevention services.

Finally, and most important, the two businesses are characterized by very different cash flows. Response generates erratic inflows, while Prevention generates predictable, recurring revenues. Response's annual cash flow typically comes from only a few sources, while Prevention's comes from many customers, each contributing a small portion of the total. Response's cash flow comes from different customers each year. Prevention's annual cash flow will come from a dynamic mix of new customers and customers from prior periods.

Response and Prevention are more than just two different businesses. They are examples of two different *business models* (Figure 1.1 below):

1. Boots and Coots' core Response business is an example of a "Pig" model (no disrespect intended). This designation refers to a business model built around large, one-time revenue streams. When the Pig business has work, cash floods in and everybody feasts.

2. Boots and Coots' Prevention unit is a "Chicken" model, generating recurring, predictable revenues (akin to eggs) from a number of clients that each make small contributions to total annual revenues.

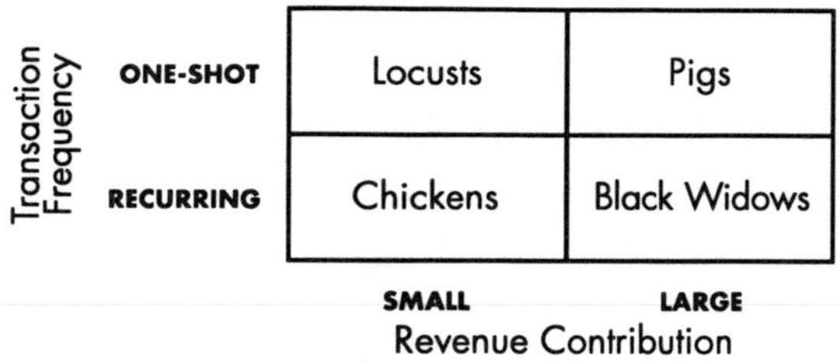

		SMALL	LARGE
Transaction Frequency	**ONE-SHOT**	Locusts	Pigs
	RECURRING	Chickens	Black Widows

SMALL   LARGE
Revenue Contribution

FIGURE 1.1   CHICKENS & PIGS FRAMEWORK

MODEL FEATURES

Simply put, a company's business model is an entity that generates different types of revenue streams. The axes that define Figure 1.1, revenue contribution and transaction frequency, each have distinct behavioral dimensions. Thus, business models are more than simply descriptors of cash flows.

Revenue Contribution

Revenue contribution answers a "distributional" question: Does the business have customers who make "significant" contributions to total revenues? The revenue contribution feature depicts annual revenues and reveals whether one or more customers contributed unusually large portions. Revenue contribution is not measured in dollars.

This point is so important and subtle that an illustrative example is warranted. Consider the case of two automobile dealers. Each sells an average of one car per day, or 365 cars per year. Each sells only to individual customers; no customer buys more than one car in any given year. One dealer specializes in small cars and receives an average of $20,000 per car. The other is a high-end retailer and receives an average of $50,000 per vehicle.

While the dollar values of the transactions are significantly different, the dealers are identical in terms of the revenue contribution they experience. Each of the two retailers' customers contributes the same amount (1 ÷ 365 = 0.274%) to annual sales. Both are thus Locust businesses.

"Revenue contribution" does not refer to the absolute dollars involved with the purchases. It refers instead to whether one or more individual customers make "significant," disproportionate contributions to total company revenues.[1]

In behavioral terms, the revenue contribution feature identifies a customer that the company finds virtually impossible to refuse. The revenue contribution feature has many forms in a wide variety of business models. Consider the following three examples:

1. One of my former clients had only one customer.
2. Roughly 90 percent of wheel manufacturer Superior Industries' (NYSE: SUP) annual revenues come from just two customers: General Motors (NYSE: GM) and Ford (NYSE: F).
3. Two-thirds of medical-device–maker Wilson Greatbatch's (NYSE: GB) 2003 sales were to two customers, Guidant and St. Jude Medical.

The vast majority of my working students describe their employers as enterprises dominated by a small number of customers. While my northeast location undoubtedly plays a role, it's fair to say that it is common for a business to generate the bulk of its revenues from a limited number of customers.

---

[1]The Securities and Exchange Commission [SEC] says a "significant" customer is one that accounts for 10 percent or more of total sales. This figure is a pretty good approximation of the point at which a customer begins to stand out as unusually important to overall company health.

Transaction Frequency

The second axis of Figure 1.1, the transaction frequency feature, is more than just a classification tool for whether a business enjoys repeat customers. The axis categorizes businesses on the degree to which its customers are "known" and its revenues are, at the customer level, predictable.

To clarify the point, let's use examples we all know well. My wife used to go to our local grocery store (XYZ) an average of three or four times each week. Her visits to XYZ have declined recently because she has started to frequent another grocery (ABC) that has just opened near our home. Has the manager of XYZ store called my wife to ask why she is visiting the store less often? No. Has anybody at XYZ store noticed that my wife's weekly purchases have dropped by about 25 percent? No. Has the manager of ABC store welcomed my wife as a new customer? No. As often as she shops at these stores, my wife is anonymous to the retailers.

The grocery stores may know their customers' buying habits and preferences, but their knowledge is statistical. The customer they know is a profile of their "average" customer. Sophisticated grocers may have multiple profiles, but they don't know my wife.

Technologic change would seem to be altering this picture. My wife uses a bonus card whenever she visits the two grocers. These cards let the retailers track her purchase behavior, knowledge they use to generate targeted promotions that are mailed to our home. Does this mean the retailers now "know" my wife?

But even such sophisticated data collection changes nothing strategically. The grocers can still only make statistical predictions regarding *when* my wife will come to their stores and *what* she will buy.

Neither grocer knows whether my wife will come at all next week, let alone how many times. The retailers' new information improves their statistical estimates to some *degree,* but it doesn't change the *kind* of knowledge they have of my wife. She's still anonymous to both.

Similarly, Wal-Mart "knows" that the average credit card customer returns to its store six times per month. It knows the days and times of the week when store traffic is highest and so can set staffing levels accordingly. However, its customer knowledge is only statistical. Wal-Mart may have state-of-the-art data on customer behavior, but it cannot predict when my wife or I will come to the store or what we will buy. They don't even know which store we will visit.

Returning to Figure 1.1, "recurring transactions" are customer-specific and highly certain. If the business has recurring transactions, someone in the organization can say, "We know that we will do business with customer DEF next month. We know what we're going to do with the customer. We're at least 95 percent confident that all of our predictions relating to customer DEF are accurate." If such knowledge and certainty are absent, the business does not enjoy recurring transactions.

In some cases, that knowledge may be principal-to-principal—that is, owner-to-owner or CEO-to-CEO. Such knowledge is often delegated, however. Payroll services provider Paychex (NASDAQ: PAYX), for example, has a customer base of 500,000 accounts. It's unrealistic to expect that the Paychex executive team has knowledge of the future buying behavior of each of these accounts. The company relies instead upon its account representatives to know what services have been delivered to a customer, whether the customer is satisfied, and the likelihood of the customer's future buying behavior.

Ideally, recurring transactions are characterized by contractual ties between the business and its customer. Cell phone providers have this type of recurring revenues, as do security services and a host of home service providers.

Some companies won't sign contracts with their partners. I know of one company that lists Wal-Mart as a recurring customer. The only contract binding the parties is a purchase order, yet the executive who runs the company knows that if he meets Wal-Mart's requirements this year, he can be 99 percent certain that Wal-Mart will be his customer again next year.

MODEL PERFORMANCE

Returning to Boots and Coots, we saw above that management chose to create an enterprise made of two parts: a Chicken (Prevention business) and a Pig (Response business). At least two other options exist that management might consider, each of which is a different business model type:

1. Using the company's demonstrated knowledge of fire suppression in the most challenging of settings, Boots and Coots might establish a branded line of fire-suppression equipment (smoke detectors, fire alarms, or fire extinguishers, for instance). The customer for this business could be the average homeowner. This type of business would generate one-time revenues (for example, a homeowner would buy a fire extinguisher), and each customer would make only tiny contributions to overall sales revenue. Referring to Figure 1.1, this would be a "Locust" business.

2. Rather than struggle to find new customers, Boots and Coots' management team might decide to work more closely with a customer it knows well and with which it enjoys a solid reputation:

Halliburton. Boots and Coots could, for example, begin to tailor its engineering unit to become Halliburton's "go-to" source for certain kinds of non-fire projects. Over time, Boots and Coots' range of capabilities could be expanded, each time gaining new Halliburton projects. Halliburton's revenue contribution would constitute an enormous portion of Boots and Coots' total sales, but the flow would be recurring (albeit from different Halliburton projects).

As Halliburton became more and more important to Boots and Coots, the question of who is "master" of the relationship would become increasingly problematic. In this model, Boots and Coots would be building its business around one customer; saying "no" to Halliburton would be almost impossible. Boots and Coots would be a captive of its customer and vulnerable to any swings in the customer's demands. That's why, as indicated in Figure 1.1, this business model is called a "Black Widow."

Which of these choices is best? While many variables must be considered, earnings potential should be a key factor in deciding between the Chicken, Pig, Locust, and Black Widow models.

Looking at Table 1.3 below, we see that

- Chicken businesses (like Boots and Coots' Prevention business) have the highest gross and net margins;
- Black Widow businesses' gross margins are low because the customers set the purchase price;
- Pig businesses' earnings (like those of Boots and Coots' Response business) are boom-and-bust, with strongly positive and strongly negative years contained in the average figures; and
- Locust businesses' low gross margins force them to be as cost conscious as Black Widows.

TABLE 1.3 AVERAGE FINANCIAL PERFORMANCE BY MODEL TYPE

	CHICKEN	PIG	LOCUST	BLACK WIDOW
	LIFELINE (NASDAQ:LIFE) ADP (NYSE:ADP)	KORN FERRY (NYSE:KFY) KEANE (NYSE:KEA)	KROGER (NYSE:KR) WAL-MART (NYSE:WM)	TODD SHIPYARDS (NYSE:TOD) VISTEON (NYSE:VC)
Gross margin	53.3	33.1	24.4	17.1
Net margin	10.5	-0.3	2.4	1.6

(All figures %. This table was computed by collecting the earnings for the identified companies for the past five years. Reported figures are averages of each category's exemplars.)

Boots and Coots' management team chose to retain and emphasize the company's Prevention business. As Table 1.3 suggests, this is the decision that holds the greatest earnings potential. As we'll see in Chapter 4, this decision is also consistent with the best way to cure an ailing business. From anecdotal evidence and my consulting experience, Boots and Coots will be "fixed" when its Prevention business represents at least 30 percent of total (non-Halliburton) revenues.

SUMMARY

The easiest way to view business models—and the most intuitive—is to see them as sources of different types of revenue streams. This chapter categorized these revenue flows on two dimensions: whether or not the revenues *recur* from one time period to the next, and the *number of sources* that provide the revenues. From these dimensions, we saw that four different business model types can be identified, each with unique earnings potential.

Perhaps paradoxically, the axes used to classify the business models are more important than the model types themselves. The revenue-recurrence axis introduces a *behavioral* dimension to business models. This dimension has two layers.

On one hand, the behavioral dimension touches upon whether the company has a stable, financially productive relationship with its customers. A visit to a local bookstore will quickly uncover a number of books that suggest all businesses should have relationships with all customers. This chapter suggests that such thinking is simplistic. Locusts and Pigs do not, by design, have ongoing relationships with their customers.

A second facet of the behavioral element involves you, the strategic decision maker. Recurring relationships are, by definition, "certain." You know the customer; you know how to satisfy and keep him or her as a customer. This customer's revenue is so predictable that you can leverage it to generate current cash from a lending institution. Having this customer gives you choices: you can maintain your business conservatively, or you can be aggressive. If aggressiveness leads to trouble, this customer's presence allows you to recover by returning to a conservative posture.

The second axis, revenue contribution, introduces *hierarchy* into strategy formulation. A hierarchy establishes that some customers can be more important than others. At one extreme are the customers that a company *cannot afford to lose;* at the other extreme are the customers that a company *expects to lose* once money has crossed the table.

Customer hierarchy is thus intimately tied to *dependence.* In those cases where dependence upon one or more customers is present, management almost always strives to prevent the loss of the significant customer. The efforts undertaken to retain the customer become part of the organization's strategy. The larger the customer's revenue contribution, the more that company's strategy is built around him or her. So it's fair to say, all else being equal, that the presence of a significant customer reduces a company's degrees of strategic freedom.

For companies that don't have customers who make individually significant contributions to overall revenues, strategy is relatively unconstrained. The loss of a customer won't be noticeably harmful to the company's financial performance. Customer loss is an outcome that isn't feared; it may, in fact, be desired. The absence of any significant customer gives management the greatest degree of strategic freedom: management can take the company in any direction it wants to go.

The axes used to categorize business models are subtle and complex. When I show them the matrix in Figure 1.1, most executives try to classify their companies immediately (e.g., "We're a Locust-business"). My counsel is to proceed more slowly and examine their company in terms of the main axes.

The thesis of this chapter is that all businesses can be categorized on a simple, two-by-two matrix. Yet, we all *know* the world is too complex to facilitate such a simple classification. You'll be better served if you first develop an understanding of your business model in terms of the axes. Only then will it be appropriate to classify your business within the C&P—or any—framework.

2

Strategic DNA

Business models are not predetermined by environment or structure. Management chooses the business model(s) the company will operate. If management chooses well, the business has a head start on success, and strategy will be relatively easy. If management chooses poorly, the business isn't necessarily doomed, but a poor business model makes success much harder to achieve and even harder to maintain. In this chapter, we'll examine the choices that create a business model.

BUILDING BLOCKS

Business models are created by three explicit, closely tied identification choices made by top management (see Figure 2.1): customer to be served, value proposition to be offered, and resources and capabilities to be used to create and deliver the value proposition.

"Core competencies" are the currently popular starting point for business creation. That businesses should create new businesses by leveraging what they do best has become a widely adopted notion. Unfortunately, it's wrong.

FIGURE 2.1 BUSINESS MODEL ELEMENTS

The admonition at the root of this notion ("Don't get into businesses you don't know how to manage.") is correct. The track record of failed diversification efforts offers ample evidence of this. In logic terms, the equation would be written as A –> B, where A is unfamiliarity with the new domain, and B is business failure. The advice "Begin with what you know" rests on the assumption that by negating A you also negate B. That's a difficult logical leap to make: knowing a domain doesn't always lead to business success. The lesson of almost all the failed dot.com start-ups is that great resources don't necessarily result in viable businesses.

To define a business, begin by identifying its customer.

Customers & Customer Pools

Customers, whether individuals or other businesses, are the source of a business's revenues. Customers receive the invoices; they pay the bills.

This seems self-evident. But executives, academics, and journalists often lose sight of the customer when they describe a business and its strategies, falling into the trap of thinking of the end-user as the customer. A toy manufacturer may regard the child who plays with the toy as the customer, but unless the toy maker sold the item directly to the child's parents, and invoiced the parents, the child is not the customer. The child's parents probably purchased the toy from a store. If the toy maker sold and invoiced the store for the toys it manufactured, the store is the customer; if the toy store purchased the toy from a distributor, the toy maker's customer is the distributor. Business models are built around customers, not end-users.

The total number of active customers comprise a business's *customer pool*. An active customer is one that has provided revenue during what the business defines as its "current time period." A customer is active even if it hasn't yet contributed revenues but is contractually bound to do so during the current time period. For some businesses, the relevant current time period is weekly (e.g., a grocery store). For others, the period is monthly (e. g., a utility), quarterly, or yearly (e.g., a publicly traded manufacturing company).

If a customer doesn't meet either of the conditions that allow it to be classified as active, the customer is classified as *lost*. In some cases, a lost customer can be reacquired. Some businesses live a constant cycle of customer reacquisition and loss. (A final category, the *prospective* customer, is the marketer's concern and not germane to this discussion.)

Pool Size

Each business model type is associated with active customer pools of different sizes, as shown in Figure 2.2 below.

Locust businesses have enormous customer pools. Archetypal Locust businesses like Amazon.com (NASDAQ: AMZN) and Wal-Mart (NYSE: WMT) have customer pools measured in the tens of millions.

Black Widow businesses have very small customer pools. At the extreme, a Black Widow business can survive with only one customer.

More commonly, Black Widows have one or two key customers and a small number of minor customers. Wheel manufacturer Superior Industries (NYSE: SUP), for example, has two key customers (GM and Ford). Together they account for about 90 percent of Superior's sales. An estimated 10 companies generate the remaining 10 percent of Superior's total revenues.

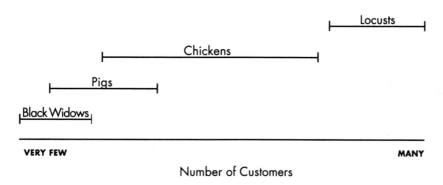

FIGURE 2.2   RELATIVE NUMBER OF CUSTOMERS BY MODEL TYPE

Pig businesses have larger customer pools than Black Widows, but their customer pools are generally small. Jacobs Engineering (NYSE: JEC), for example, has a customer pool of roughly 40 to 50 accounts. FTI Consulting (NYSE: FCN), one of America's leading forensic accounting and litigation support specialists, sells its services to about 1,200 clients.

Chicken businesses have larger customer pools than Black Widows, but pool size varies widely. Hewitt Associates' (NYSE: HEW) Chicken business, for example, has only 300 customers, while Paychex (NASDAQ: PAYX), a payroll services provider, has a client pool of 500,000 companies.

Pool Stability

Pool stability refers to the number of successive time periods a customer remains active. By definition, *stable* customer pools have customers who remain active for many successive time periods. These stable relationships can be either formal (where the parties are bound by contracts that are renewed) or informal (where no contracts exist but the relationship endures).

Unstable customer pools are volatile. Because customers active in one period are often lost in the next, the composition of unstable customer pools changes radically from period to period.

As shown in Figure 2.3, pool stabilities vary by business model.

The Value Proposition

The purpose of a business is to help customers solve problems. The *value proposition* represents solutions a business offers customers.

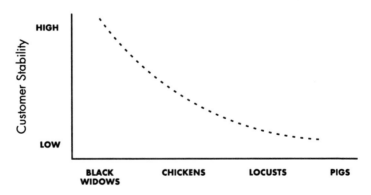

FIGURE 2.3   CUSTOMER POOL STABILITY OF MODEL TYPES

While customer circumstances are unique from one situation to the next, their problem types (and the solutions required) correspond to the type of business model shown below in Figure 2.4.

Chickens & Pigs

Locusts **PREVENT**	Pigs **SOLVE**
Chickens **MANAGE**	Black Widows **PARTNER**

FIGURE 2.4   SOLUTIONS BY MODEL TYPE

The business's product or service is part of its value proposition, but it's rarely the only (or the most important) aspect of that proposition. A *compelling* value proposition has both *tangible* (the product or service) and *intangible* (customer assurance) elements.

Pig Business Value Propositions

"We've designed and installed fire-suppression systems for restaurants of all types. We can do the same for you." *(A Buffalo-area fire-suppression specialty company)*

"We have helped countless businesses take their businesses online. We can do the same for you." *(IBM Business Services)*

"We have the passion and creativity you want, and the resources the job needs. We can be the florist for your upcoming wedding." *(A local florist)*

Pig businesses deal in solutions that solve the customer's problem fully and completely: buildings are designed, bridges erected, systems installed. Pig businesses always provide a clear and decisive project end point at which both parties know the work has been completed. Once this point is reached, business between the Pig business and its customer ceases.

Chicken Business Value Propositions

"We'll handle every aspect of your payroll for you, from processing and delivering the weekly paychecks to preparing all of the employees' tax forms. We'll handle your payroll matters more effectively and more efficiently than you ever could. The process will be so smooth and transparent that the only time you'll remember we're doing it for you is when you compute the savings we generate every pay period." *(Payroll providers like ADP and Paychex)*

"Our items will be shipped on time and in the exact quantities you ordered (our fill rates will be 100 percent). We'll manage the displays for you. We'll present the items in a good-better-best arrangement, inducing customers to trade up to the higher price-points. At the end of the financial period, you'll be delighted with the dollars per square foot our displays generated for you." *(Newell to discount retailers like Wal-Mart and Target)*

"Our products will help you sell your products. Retailers that you sell to will find that computers fitted with our latest microprocessor will jump off their shelves. We'll make you look like a hero to your customer: he'll make money by carrying your product line. You won't be able to keep up with all the orders he'll be giving you." *(Intel, to the computer manufacturers that sell their finished goods through retail sales channels)*

Chicken businesses do more than just solve the customer's immediate problem. They *manage* issues relating to the problems' recurrence, in effect taking responsibility for all matters relating to the problem. If handled properly, a Chicken business's work is unobtrusive and transparent: the customer sees no glitches and only notices the Chicken business when it's time to issue payment. When a Chicken business is serving its customer well, the payment the customer makes to the Chicken business is the easiest check for it to write.

Locust Business Value Propositions

"Our prices are the lowest in the area; you won't find a better price if you try. We have all the national brands. Our stock is constantly changing; you won't be bored by seeing last year's items. We're easy to deal with: we have plenty of parking and a 100 percent satisfaction guarantee." *(Wal-Mart)*

"We have the most complete range of items you could want, including the most esoteric of titles. We make it easy to choose by offering online reviews written by readers like you. Our costs are low because we have no rent to pay. We won't charge you sales tax, and we'll cover the shipping costs if you buy more than one or two items." *(Amazon.com books)*

Locust businesses are not close to their customers, who are transient and anonymous. A Locust business simply has too many customers to keep track of them all, and in terms of revenue and profit contribution, no customer is important enough to merit special attention or a customized solution. Customers are "known" statistically; large Locust businesses use market research to generate profiles of their "average" customers.

Locust businesses offer value propositions aimed relatively low, striving to make it easy for customers to do business with them. *Simplification* is most often achieved by bundling a range of solutions to small problems that might otherwise deter a customer from choosing them. No single solution offered by a Locust is critical in itself because that particular solution is likely to be critical only to a subset of customers; bundling solutions insures that Locust businesses will be able to meet a broad range of needs and concerns of the masses.

Black Widow Business Value Propositions

"We'll adopt the quality program you want us to employ, even though the cost will strain our resources both financially and in terms of personnel. Indeed, we'll join you down the whole quality and efficiency journey: we'll be with you when, three years from now, you evaluate whether QS-9000 has improved overall delivered quality; we'll be there when you develop remedies to related problems none of us can at this stage foresee; and we'll join you in whatever solutions you mandate." *(Auto parts supplier to its automobile manufacturing customer)*

"We'll begin using Radio Frequency Identification Devices (RFIDs) in the shipments we send you, and we'll absorb all of the related costs. As was the case when we did what you requested and introduced electronic data exchange (EDI) to exchange information between your computers and ours, we'll share our experiences with the new RFID technology with you." *(A supplier to Wal-Mart)*

Black Widow businesses participate in initiatives the customer has put on the table. Indeed, the Black Widow business will become a full participant in those initiatives even in those cases where the customer has little more than a vague idea where its initiative will lead.

In essence, Black Widow businesses partner with their customers, joining them at every step of an often uncertain journey.

Value Propositions: Summary

Value propositions are solutions to customer problems. Different business models offer different solutions.

As suggested by the preceding examples, the difference between a good value proposition and a compelling one is the degree to which the customer's emotions are addressed. Compelling value propositions fully embrace the customer's fears and concerns.

Customers don't always have elevated fears and concerns. Locust customers generally want "frictionless" transactions that proceed quickly and with as few disruptions as possible. If the Locust business fails to meet these customer expectations (by burdening customers with chronic parking problems or long checkout lines, for instance), the Locust customer simply will not come back.

For customers of the other business model types, however, the emotional considerations are more substantive. To one degree or another, accepting the value proposition means the customer must trust the solution-provider. Compelling value propositions offer solutions that both resolve the customer's problem *and* reassure the customer of the credibility of the promised solution.

Resources and Capabilities

A company's *resources and capabilities* create and deliver the value proposition. Resources and capabilities are thus the means by which the promises made to a customer are kept.

Locusts **SCALE**	Pigs **NETWORK**
Chickens **STANDARDIZATION**	Black Widows **COMPETENCE**

FIGURE 2.5   RESOURCE ORIENTATIONS BY MODEL TYPE

While each company is likely to have its own unique set of resources and capabilities, the nature of the value proposition pulls the resources in directions specific to the business model. These broad orientations are summarized below.

Pig Business Resources and Capabilities

A florist who wants to do business with a local funeral home must put together a picture book showing the different arrangements it's ready to deliver. That book is left with the mortician. It may be months before the mortuary calls with an order, and the likelihood that the florist will have on-hand the raw materials needed to complete the customer's order will almost certainly be zero. The florist needs a network of suppliers from whom urgently needed materials can be obtained.

Boots and Coots' Response unit is similarly situated. The company's long-standing practice of laying off idle employees makes it likely that needed resources will not be in place at the moment a client calls with an oil-well fire emergency. Boots and Coots must draw upon a network of potential employees if it is to assemble a Response team quickly.

The unpredictable nature of a Pig business's demand, coupled with the unique nature of each Pig project, means a Pig business is seldom fully prepared when a customer appears on the doorstep. A Pig business must maintain a network of sources from which it can draw high-quality resources, usually on short notice.

Chicken Business Resources and Capabilities

When Lifeline (NASDAQ: LIFE) signs on a new customer, that customer accepts the company's promise that it will respond immediately when called upon, regardless of day or time of the health event. When Boots and Coots signs up a Prevention customer, the promise binding the parties is that Boots and Coots will dispatch to the client's site trained and accredited people who will meet the customer's insurance needs.

Chicken businesses make promises to their customers regarding both present and future performance. Customers assess the robustness of the future-performance promise by assessing the Chicken business's present performance. If the Chicken business fulfills its present promises, the customer accepts the likelihood that future-performance promises will be kept. Conversely, a present-period failure raises doubts about the delivery of any future-performance promises.

When a Chicken business loses a customer, it loses an annuity stream. Chicken businesses therefore have a large stake in maintaining consistently flawless performance so that customers are retained from period to period. They strive to employ processes that perform without variation, time after time. As a result, Chicken businesses tend to standardize and formalize (document procedures and guidelines) their internal operations. All else being equal, Chicken businesses are the business model type least likely to embrace change and innovation.

Locust Business Resources & Capabilities

In 2005, more than 130 million customers visited Wal-Mart stores every week. To handle customer numbers like these, Wal-Mart owns and operates almost 6,000 stores worldwide (totaling 663 million square feet of selling space). Its fixed assets are valued at $84 billion.

The story is similar at the Home Depot (NYSE: HD). To handle the roughly 1.3 billion customers who moved through its cash registers in 2004, Home Depot owns and operates roughly 173 million square feet of retail space and has fixed assets valued at $28.4 billion.

As these examples suggest, Locust businesses make fixed-cost investments sufficient to handle the enormous number of customers they serve and to process the enormous number of transactions these customers generate. (All else being equal, Locust businesses are more likely to invest in extensive information technology [IT] systems than other business models.) These investments make this business model type particularly sensitive to capacity utilization. Locust businesses live in a world of break-even points and constant cost concerns.

Black Widow Business Resources & Capabilities

Black Widow businesses depend upon a very small number of customers for the vast majority of their revenues. This dependency affects their resources and capabilities in two ways. First, Black Widow businesses rely heavily upon current-period execution as their best means of ensuring retention of the customer for the future. The ongoing, often high-volume, nature of the customer requirements allow for the development of "core competencies" that improve process execution in terms of both effectiveness and efficiency.

Second, and even more significant, Black Widow businesses frequently make internal investments that move them in support of their customers' latest initiatives. When automobile manufacturers mandated the adoption of the QS-9000 quality initiative in the mid-1990s, for example, each affected supplier was forced to incur compliance and verification costs that averaged about $120,000.

Black Widow businesses are far less resistant to change than the typical Chicken business. The Black Widow business needs to incorporate customer-mandated changes into its existing core competencies. Black Widow businesses as a result are the model type most likely to allocate internal resources and develop internal practices to create a "learning organization."

INTERCONNECTED THREADS

We've been considering the three elements of business models separately, but customers, value propositions, and resources and capabilities also work with one another, in *paired* and *triangular* interactions. Each paired interaction is the basis for specific business model properties. Together, the three elements create an entity that is very difficult to change.

Customer/Value Proposition

The business model type (Chicken, Pig, Locust, Black Widow) results from a paired interaction of customer and value proposition.

For example, consider two companies: Palm (NASDAQ: PALM) and Research in Motion (NASDAQ: RIMM). Both are "high-tech" companies with business models constructed around a proprietary hand-held electronic device. (Palm created the Palm Pilot, an electronic organizer; RIMM created the Blackberry, a device that allows the user to receive and send e-mail messages wirelessly, without connection to a computer.)

Palm's founders expressly wanted to have their device in virtually everybody's hands. Successive generations of the device offered new features and enhancements to existing features. Palm offers devices across a range of price points in order to attract buyers of all types, from the entry-level college students to "power users."

RIMM built a different model. They sold to corporations rather than to individuals, offering a subscription service with pricing based on factors such as the number of end-users and volume of messages delivered.

Palm's customer/value proposition combination created a Locust business; RIMM's customer/value proposition combination created a Chicken business.

Value Proposition/Resources & Capabilities

A business model's profitability is a function of its value proposition and its resources and capabilities.

Pricing is a value proposition element. In general, compelling value propositions command higher prices than non-compelling value propositions. However, a high price doesn't always result in a high profit margin. Compelling value propositions may be more expensive to produce or deliver than less compelling ones. The efficiency of a business—how it uses its available resources to create or deliver the value proposition—significantly influences achieved profitability margins.

In general, business models with high fixed costs have the most problems with resource utilization: efficiency in one period is often hard to reproduce in the next.

Customer/Resources & Capabilities

The size of the business model is a function of the customer and the nature of its resources and capabilities. "Large" business models

- serve a large customer pool;
- have extensive marketing systems to communicate with customers;
- make large investments to develop, create, and deliver their value propositions; and
- employ sophisticated control systems to monitor internal performance.

These factors suggest that, all else being equal, larger models require more "professional" management than smaller models.

The history of Dell, Inc. (NASDAQ: DELL), illustrates this. Michael Dell started the company in his dorm room in 1983, buying computer components from IBM dealers and then reselling them by advertising in newspapers and computer magazines. When his business hit $80,000 per month in 1984, he dropped out of school and devoted all his attention to it.

In 1988, Dell began selling to large customers, including government agencies. The company opened international offices and started selling Dell-branded PCs in retail locations like Staples (NASDAQ: SPLS). As the model grew, so too did a range of internal problems and costs. Company warehouses were overstocked; new product development was plagued by costly errors. Profits fell 64 percent in 1990.

Dell responded by professionalizing his management team. He hired experienced executives from Motorola (NYSE: MOT), Hewlett Packard (NYSE: HPQ), and Apple Computer (NASDAQ: AAPL). The executives brought with them skills in operations, new product development, and finance.

The Rigid Triangle

Business models evolve over time. Value propositions are refined as competitors present their own offerings to customers. Resources and capabilities are enhanced through learning and modified as the value proposition changes. The business model size changes as the size of the customer pool expands or shrinks. Replacing any one of the three elements will, by definition, necessitate change in the other two elements. Customers cannot be changed without changing the value proposition and the resources and capabilities. A new value proposition will inevitably involve changing both the customer base and the resources and capabilities.

Business models change in an evolutionary, incremental manner. Radical or revolutionary business model change is virtually impossible to achieve. Indeed, management usually lacks the freedom to make all the changes it wishes to. Commitments to customers, and to communities in which customers are located, are difficult to break. If the company and its customers are bound by contracts, change is even more difficult.

Ongoing commitments to employees and other resource providers also constrain management's ability to make radical changes. Management cannot just abandon old resources and capabilities—a rule well understood by managers in industries where pension plans and health care costs for retired employees represent a chronic and growing drain on finances. In fact, management frequently resists even the *idea* of a radical change in their business model. When their businesses get into trouble, managers generally try to repair, rather than change, their model.

Underlying this managerial preference is the nature of strategy development. Business models become domains in which strategists learn virtually all their business's strategic variables. They come to know their customers' expectations, learn how to overcome the internal problems that continually crop up, and build market intelligence about their rivals, including details regarding the value propositions these competitors are offering to prospective customers. The business model becomes a refuge, a domain of "created certainty" in a turbulent world. The longer an executive inhabits this domain, the more uncertain and intimidating a new business model appears.

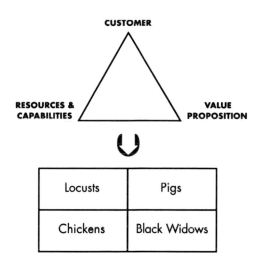

FIGURE 2.6 SUMMARY OF CHAPTER 2

So, because of wide ranging structural, behavioral, and decisional factors, strategists tend to resist changing their business model. It's fair to say that, once selected, the three business model elements are permanent for any given company.

SUMMARY

The essence of this chapter's argument is illustrated below.

Business models (Chickens, Pigs, Locusts, Black Widows) are created by managerial choice. Every company operates at least one business model, and every such model is one of the four types diagrammed in Figure 2.6 and described in Chapter 1.

Once a business model is created, behavioral conditions render it a permanent structure. If the point is reached at which a business model proves to be untenable, management is unable to simply change the model into a more favorable type. If management initially created a Pig business, the business will remain a Pig.

Strategies bring a business model to life. In the terms identified in the Introduction, strategies implement the business model, providing the means by which the company finds customers, presents its value proposition to them, and creates and delivers the value proposition purchased by the customer.

As we'll see in the next chapter, the strategies a company pursues are directly influenced by the business model type being put into operation.

3

Competitive Strategy

Just as the customer is the starting point for building a business model, the customer is at the center of competitive strategy.[2] Competition is a contest over who "wins" the customer. In some cases, the victory is long lived because the customer does not return again to the market for many years. In other cases, the victory is temporary and the customer is back in the market quickly, sparking a new competitive battle. The customer may be a source of revenue for many successive time periods. In other cases, the customer's revenue comes only once.

Whatever the nature of the victory, the process is the same: the customer weighs the value propositions of the competing companies and selects one. The customer determines the winner of all competitive battles.

CUSTOMERS AND COMPETITIVE STRATEGY

Customers are the fundamental focus of competitive strategy. This statement might not be "in sync" with how you think of competitive strategy. The traditional, "product-oriented" perspective on competi-

---

[2]In this chapter I use the term "competitive strategy" as a synonym for "business-level strategy." The terms are interchangeable.

tive strategy generally regards new products, bundled services, discounted prices, and the like as the key variables in any competitive strategy. From a business model perspective, though, these product and service elements are all simply aspects of the value proposition. Strategy academics have learned, and have issued warnings for many years, that a product-oriented perspective is an incomplete way to approach and manage strategy.

Contemporary strategic management regards "resources and capabilities" as the key variables. While they are certainly components of a business model, resources and capabilities are critical only in the context of the value proposition they create and deliver. They are necessary, but not sufficient, for strategic success.

Another "traditional" perspective of competitive strategy focuses upon the industry in which competition takes place and the rivals one meets there. Here the focus is on the competitors and the field of play. This perspective does not describe the *objective* of the battle—that is, what the competing entities are fighting over and striving to win.

Earnings are commonly used as a "final score" measure of a competition's outcome. The winner, goes the reasoning, earns more than the loser.

I don't see earnings as the game's score. To me, they are the trophy awarded after the game is over. Earnings are not the prize waiting on the other side of the goal line, nor are they the result of touching home plate or shooting the puck past the goaltender.

A fundamental axiom of competitive strategy is this: *a company doesn't win earnings, it wins customers.*

Customers provide the company with its revenue. Earnings come *after* the customers have been won and *after* the revenues have been received. Earnings are an accounting artifact, a figure that's computed, a box score for rumination. Earnings are what remain once the costs, including those related to winning the customers, have been deducted.

Customers are the fundamental focus of competitive strategy. Without them, there are neither revenues nor earnings.

CUSTOMER POOLS

Chapter 2 introduced the concept of the customer pool, the group of active customers with which a company does business.

The customer pool affords a strategic, high-level view of a company's customers; it's where a strategist looks to get an overview of a company's customers. The customer pool identifies the *type of customer* (Chicken, for example) a company serves. (Finer details like the customers' gender, income, and age are generally the realm of marketing specialists.)

Customer pools are *homogeneous,* composed of a single customer-type. All companies have at least one customer pool.[3]

As described in Chapter 2, the size of a customer pool varies from one type of business model to the next. Locust businesses have the largest customer pools; Black Widow businesses tend to have small ones. (See Figure 2.2.)

This doesn't mean that businesses of the same model type necessarily have customer pools of the same size. Two Chicken businesses that operate in the same industry, for instance, may have customer pools of significantly different sizes. *Management preference* influences the size of a company's customer pool.

Indeed, the size of a company's customer pool is *controllable,* something management can shape and influence. Management can choose

---

[3]Companies can have more than one customer pool. We will explore multiple customer pools in Chapter 4.

to either *increase* or *decrease* the size of its customer pool. For example, Home Depot (NYSE: HD), a very successful Locust business, has been expanding its customer pool by about 20 percent each year since the early 1990s. In contrast, Best Buy (NYSE: BBY), another Locust business, embarked in 2004 upon a program of eliminating from its pool those customers who pursue price discounts too aggressively. That group may be as large as 20 percent of the company's 500 million customers.

Management also controls the *pace* at which the size of the customer pool is changed. *Organic change* is the relatively slow process of acquiring customers by means of engaging in competitive, marketplace actions or eliminating customers by means of attrition. *Quantum change* is the rapid addition or elimination of customers through acquisitions or divestitures.

As suggested by Figure 3.1 below, customer pools may be regarded as a type of *stock* with *inflows* and *outflows*.

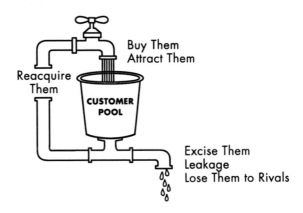

FIGURE 3.1 CUSTOMER POOLS INFLOW AND OUTFLOW

It is the role of competitive strategy to regulate the flows into and out of the customer pool. Specifically, competitive strategy is concerned with acquiring new customers, retaining those currently held, and reacquiring those that have been lost.

Customer Pool Inflows

A company can follow two paths to increase the number of customers it serves. It can try to attract them with a compelling value proposition, an organic approach predicated upon winning competitive battles. Or it can obtain clients at a quantum pace by acquiring a rival, a corporate strategy known as "horizontal integration." As shown by the following examples, both approaches are expensive:

1. Starbucks (NASDAQ: SBUX) announced an organic growth plan to expand its number of stores from the 2004 level of 8,600 to 30,000 worldwide. Each new store costs Starbucks roughly $600,000. Local marketing costs to win the competitive battles will accrue on top of this initial cost per store.

2. When Adelphia Communications went into Chapter 11 bankruptcy protection, potential acquirers (looking for quantum growth) attached a value of roughly $3,500 to each of Adelphia's subscribers. At $70 to $75 per month, each customer represented roughly four years of revenue. Adelphia had approximately 5 million subscribers.

Customer Pool Outflows

Customer loss can be either *deliberate* (e.g., refusing to sell to certain customers or divesting units that serve particular groups of customers) or *unintentional* (e.g., inadvertently losing them to rivals).

Customer loss can also be *structural*—that is, related to the type of business model the company operates. The one-shot business models (Locusts or Pigs) lose 100 percent of their customers once their dealings with their clients are completed. Speaking metaphorically, there's a hole in the bottom of these businesses' customers pools, and 100 percent of their customers leak through that hole.

COMPETITIVE STRATEGY AND CUSTOMER POOLS

As previously noted, a customer pool's inflows and outflows are managed by competitive strategy. Because the customer pool of each type of business model evolves in its own distinctive way, the competitive strategy and practices used to meet the challenges is specific to the type of business model.

Chicken Business Competitive Strategy

While some customers are inevitably lost, or "leak," from the pool, Chicken businesses are generally able to hold onto their customers from one period to the next. Chicken businesses have relatively stable customer pools: new customers are added to a preexisting base. The result is a customer pool that, over time, looks like this:

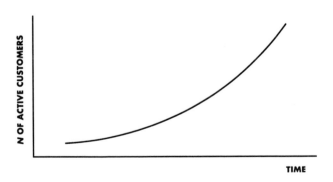

FIGURE 3.2   CHICKEN BUSINESS CUSTOMER POOLS OVER TIME

This stability gives Chicken businesses the potential to build relatively large customer pools. Advanced Data Processing (NYSE: ADP), for example, has a customer pool of five hundred thousand clients. Its customer pool is remarkably stable: an average payroll services customer remains within it for eight years.

Competitive strategy for a Chicken business is to *accumulate customers* (Figure 3.3). Customer accumulation involves efforts to acquire new customers and aggressively retain current customers.

Payroll services provider Paychex (NASDAQ: PAYX) is a company that has generally acquired its customers organically, by engaging rivals in markets and winning customers one at a time. Its customer curve looks very similar to Figure 3.2.

Cox Communications (NYSE: COX), by contrast, acquired most of its customers through horizontal integration (by acquiring rivals). While similar to that shown in Figure 3.2, Cox's customer pool shows marked "steps" that correspond to sudden inflows of acquired customers.

To a Chicken business, customers are annuities, a stream of future revenues and earnings. Chicken businesses thus have a very significant stake in retaining each of their customers. This affects a Chicken business's competitive strategy in two ways:

1. It places a premium on fulfillment of the value proposition promised to current customers as a means of customer retention.
2. It slows the pace at which new customers are added. Since new customers must not come at the expense of diminishing the service to existing customers, Chicken businesses must expand capacity *before* adding new customers. Budgetary discipline limits the extent of such speculative investments in expanding capacity, thereby constraining the rate at which new customers can be added.

ADP is a good example of such constrained, regulated growth. The company grew its customer pool at a modest but steady rate of about six percent per year between 1993 and 2002.

Chicken businesses often balance the constrained pace of adding new customers by increasing the revenue flow associated with the customers they have. Paychex and Cox both use this method to increase revenues faster than customer growth. Each sells additional services to existing customers, turning a single customer into a source of multiple revenue streams.

Pig Business Competitive Strategy

The Pig business's customer pool is the most unstable of the four model types. As shown below in Figure 3.3, the number of customers in a Pig business's customer pool varies widely from period to period. Recall that a Pig business's product or service is the complete solution to a customer's problem—typically delivered as a *project*—developed and delivered within a specified time period.

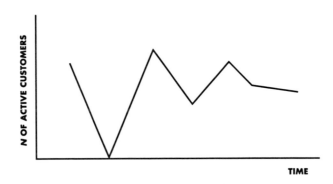

FIGURE 3.3   PIG BUSINESS CUSTOMER POOLS OVER TIME

The Pig business's customer pool volatility is a function of the size of the project the Pig business tries to obtain. In general, the larger the project, the fewer are available at any point in time. For example, only a limited number of bridges are currently being built, and there are fewer commercial dams under construction.

Pig businesses survive dry spells between large projects by taking on smaller projects that can be backlogged, thereby providing work for successive time periods. The customer pool rises significantly when small projects are used to fill "idle time."[4]

When a large project comes onto the market and the Pig business develops quotations and marketing materials to try to secure the contract, the order backlog is reduced to free up resources that will, the owner hopes, be allocated to this new contract. The customer pool drops and will stay reduced if the large contract is won.

If the contract is not won, the Pig business will try to increase the size of the customer pool with small projects, in essence repeating the cycle.

Construction company Perini (NYSE: PCR), the largest hotel and casino builder in the United States, has for over 20 years had a customer pool similar to that illustrated in Figure 3.3. Earnings, not surprisingly, swung wildly from year to year.

Reducing the wild gyrations of its customer pool is the dominant challenge of a Pig business's competitive strategy.

A particularly effective approach toward Pig business competitive strategy is a focus on *client competencies,* a strategy in which the Pig business makes itself capable of delivering a very wide range of solutions to a very narrow range of customers.

---

[4]Pig businesses frequently use price as a means of securing small projects to fill their order backlog, in effect prioritizing customer pool management over short-term profitability.

FTI Consulting (NYSE: FCN), one of America's leading forensic accounting and litigation support companies, has recently embarked upon a client competencies approach. In 2003, FTI moved to make itself a wide-ranging solutions-provider to clients (lawyers) involved in Sarbanes-Oxley–related matters. Divestitures reduced the FTI customer pool by 65 percent, but three acquisitions increased the range of capabilities it could bring to its customers. Revenue per client and earnings per client both surged.

The logic of a client competencies approach is unmistakable: while the project-type may vary from one engagement to the next, the client is the same. With one client potentially generating many different projects, client competencies is a strategy for generating repeat business, thereby partially emulating a Chicken business.

FTI illustrates the effect of the strategy. In its 2005 10K form, the company reported that 83 percent of its highly profitable 2004 revenues were generated either from repeat customers or from referrals from prior customers.

Client competencies isn't the only strategy a Pig business can employ to stabilize its customer pool. A particularly effective alternative, for those whose business suits it, is to secure *extra-long engagements*. For example, Precision controls manufacturer Moog (NYSE: MOG'A) signed a $50 million, 15-year contract with Airbus in 2004, and environmental consulting company Ecology and Environment (AMEX: EEI) obtains contracts with national governments that typically range from five to 10 years in duration. These types of contracts effectively keep the client in the Pig business's customer pool for an extended period of time. Any new customers are thus added to this stable customer base in a manner that roughly emulates that of a Chicken business.

Locust Business Competitive Strategy

Locust businesses have enormous, complex customer pools. At any point in time, their pool consists of a mixture of first-time customers and returning customers. The balance between these customer-types depends upon the business. Grocery stores, for example, have pools that are primarily returning customers. Online merchants, particularly during the dot.com boom of the late 1990s, had customer pools with a large proportion of first-time customers.

Factors such as changing customer preferences and market saturation mean that the Locust business's customer pool evolves in a pattern that mirrors the product life-cycle curve (Figure 3.4).

Krispy Kreme Doughnuts (NYSE: KKD) came to know well the curve illustrated in Figure 3.4. During its well-publicized expansion phase, new stores typically opened to an initial surge of customers. As time wore on, though, those customers became increasingly scarce.

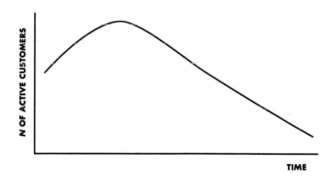

FIGURE 3.4   LOCUST BUSINESS CUSTOMER POOLS OVER TIME

Home Depot also knows the curve of Figure 3.4. An established location has a customer pool (measured as transactions per store) that declines at a rate of about three percent per year.

Overcoming the inevitable decline of the customer pool is the dominant challenge of a Locust business's competitive strategy. An approach most Locust businesses employ is to simply *add new customers* into their pool. When a Locust business moves into a market it does not yet serve, it adds that new market's customers to its customer pool. Home Depot has, for example, been adding stores (and thus customers) at a 20 percent annual pace for over 15 years, easily overwhelming its three percent annual customer leakage rate. Wal-Mart has been adding stores and square footage at a 27 percent rate since 1995. Both retailers are expanding both in the U. S. and internationally.

Locust businesses also have the capacity to bring lost customers back. Wal-Mart serves as a "best-in-class" exemplar of this capacity: on average, customers return to Wal-Mart six times per month. If the store is a super center, the average customer returns eight times per month.

This Chicken-like behavior by Locust customers is achieved through two major practices, both known to those familiar with big business and with practices that are typically part of business school curricula.

1. *Big Marketing*. By establishing and maintaining a favorable image of itself—its "brand"—the Locust business increases the chance the customer will return. Loyalty programs (the airline industry's frequent flyer programs, for example) are another marketing vehicle to create repeat customers.

2. *Innovations*. Most Locust businesses adhere to the logic behind the maxim "Innovate or die." Retailers change store layouts, formats, and/or product mix; manufacturers create new products; software-makers create upgrades. The list is endless, but the approaches all share a theme: entice the lost customers to come back by offering them a product that's "new and improved."

One of the best examples of a Locust business that survives by constant innovation is The Callaway Golf Company (NASDAQ: ELY). Callaway released its first revolutionary driver, the S2H2, in 1988. Three years later came the Big Bertha driver. In 1995, ELY released the Great Big Bertha Titanium driver. Each product was revolutionary, each offered improvements over previous products' performance, and each was ultimately widely imitated by price-cutting rivals.

The company also offers insights into the challenges of creating constant innovations:

> The biggest problem . . . is coming up with Act II. There are many companies that can introduce a [product/design] and can get a reasonable market share, but then . . . the company cannot come up with something better or something that matches the promise of the initial [product/design]. (Lal, R. and Prescott, E. D. "Callaway Golf Company." *Harvard Business School Press,* case #9-501-019, rev. February 20, 2004, 10.)

Black Widow Business Competitive Strategy

The Black Widow business customer pool is characterized by small numbers (for some companies, a single client) and an absence of new customers.

In some cases, the limited number of customers results from a lack of alternatives. Mature industries often have small total populations. For example, just 22 companies make up the entire military aircraft manufacturing sector (NAICS code #3367112). Companies that supply this industry are almost certain to be in a Black Widow situation, with total sales concentrated in their contracts with a handful of large customers.

In other cases, the small customer pool is a matter of choice. Management strikes a Faustian bargain: in exchange for recurring revenues and well-defined customer requirements, some companies make commitments to do business with a customer so large and so demanding that all others are squeezed out. Many Wal-Mart suppliers know this only too well.

As shown in Figure 3.5 below, the Black Widow business customer pool is characterized by little change. Indeed, management of the Black Widow business's customer pool is driven by a single imperative: avoid the loss of the key customer(s).

To achieve this objective, the Black Widow business's orientation is often inward; little can be gained by looking anywhere else. Black Widow businesses emphasize core competencies more than any other

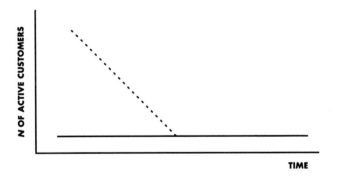

FIGURE 3.5   BLACK WIDOW BUSINESS CUSTOMER POOLS OVER TIME

model type. They focus on execution and customer requirements as the primary means of guarding against customer loss.

Growth (financial and skills-based) is achieved by *increasing the depth* of the existing customer relationships. Automobile wheel manufacturer Superior Industries (NYSE: SUP), for example, is tied to General Motors and Ford. The two auto makers represent about 90 percent of Superior's sales. For the parts maker, growth takes the form of programs given to it by its customers. As of 2004, Superior's customers had presented it with 175 unsolicited programs.

ADVANTAGE

Most companies look for an *advantage* in their competitive strategy challenges. Two types of advantage affect a company's customer pool management activities: *structural advantage* and *competitive advantage*.

Structural Advantage

Structural advantage derives from the company's business model type. A company with a structural advantage employs a type of business model that allows it to acquire and retain customers.

A company whose business model type does not let it acquire *and* retain customers is constantly burdened in its competitive endeavors:

1. A company that can *acquire* customers but cannot retain them must continually expend resources to replace and/or reacquire those customers it has lost.
2. A company that can *retain* customers but has problems obtaining new ones is vulnerable to, and dependent upon, the whims of the customers it serves.
3. A company that can *neither* acquire nor retain customers effectively or with certainty must live on the edge and scramble from opportunity to opportunity.

A company that lacks a structural advantage labors under a *structural disadvantage*. Success for these companies is hard to achieve and always short lived.

As shown in Figure 3.6, only one business model type, the Chicken, is able to both acquire and retain customers.

Competitive Advantage

A company with a *competitive advantage* offers customers a value proposition that is both inimitable and nonsubstitutable. A company possesses a competitive advantage if (a) it can address a customer problem that rivals can't address, or can address a customer problem more effectively than its rivals *and* (b) its rivals can neither copy the value proposition nor offer a reasonable alternative. For a company to enjoy a competitive advantage, both conditions must be met. The advantage disappears when rivals are able *either* to imitate the value proposition *or* to offer one comparable enough to win customers.

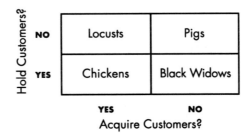

FIGURE 3.6   STRUCTURAL ADVANTAGE AND MODEL TYPE

Typically, competitive advantage is rooted in a company's resources and capabilities. *Strategic resources* are those that create a value proposition that can neither be copied nor approximated by rivals. Such resources may be tangible (a patent, for example) or intangible (knowledge of a customer's requirements).[5]

---

[5]Referring to the discussion of Chapter 2 and the related discussion of the business model triangle, competitive advantage is thus a product of the Value Proposition–Resources & Capabilities axis.

Competitive advantage may be built upon a product, an innovation, or a process. It may be based upon knowledge obtained from school, from accumulated experience, or from the intimate knowledge of a customer's requirements that results from working closely together for many years. It can be the result of holding an asset that nobody else has; it can be the result of knowing how to get the most out of a widely available resource. In short, the range of potential sources for competitive advantage is wide.

Whatever the resource that produces it, the acid test to determine whether a company has a competitive advantage is whether (a) customers embrace its value proposition and (b) rivals are unable to copy this value proposition or offer a near alternative to it.

Building a Competitive Advantage

Competitive advantage is independent of business model type. It is theoretically possible for any company, using any business model, to develop a competitive advantage.

It's common to consider one's resources and capabilities as the starting point for developing a competitive advantage. "Build advantage by enhancing your resources," goes the argument. A widely espoused variant of this is, "Core competencies—the things you do best—can become a competitive advantage."

Although widely held, this view is wide of the mark.

Spectacular competencies, core competencies, proprietary resources—they are all useless if their output is something no customer wants. Strategic resources are a *necessary* but not a *sufficient* condition for a competitive advantage. Competitive advantage requires *both* strategic resources and a compelling value proposition.

The only way to build a compelling value proposition is to start with the customer and his or her problem(s). If I brought six senior executives together and asked each of them to tell me why their customers chose their company over a rival, they would come up with at least 10 different reasons. Each reason would be the product of executive conjecture, an informed guess. And each reason would be wrong.

Few companies *really* know why their current customers selected them over their rivals because few have ever asked their customers directly.

To build a compelling value proposition, and eventually a competitive advantage, your first step is to ask your current customers what such a value proposition would look like.

Combined Advantages

Structural advantage and competitive advantage are independent of one another; a company may possess one, the other, both, or neither:

1. A Chicken business that has a competitive advantage is, theoretically, a company with a license to print money. It lives the ideal, possessing both forms of advantage.

2. A company that labors at a structural disadvantage and lacks a competitive advantage must struggle in its competitive endeavors. This company's competitive situation is reminiscent of Sisyphus, the legendary figure doomed to the fate of rolling a boulder to the top of a hill, only to see it roll back to the starting point. For such a company, competition is an endless uphill struggle.

3. The company that has a competitive advantage but lacks a structural advantage will find its competitive advantage undercut by the deficiencies of its business model:

a. The Locust business will find its compelling value proposition short lived, a victim of life-cycle tendencies inherent in Locust businesses.

b. The Pig business serves customers who have unique requirements. These customers will not find the Pig business's inimitable value proposition compelling unless it's adapted and customized to their requirements. In other words, inimitability is less relevant to customers than a solution tailored to their needs.

c. The Black Widow business will be unable to find customers who will purchase its specialized value proposition.

4. The company that has a structural advantage but lacks a competitive advantage will earn less than rivals that have both, but the company should still be able to succeed financially. Companies with a structural advantage are designed to win.

SUMMARY

This chapter's core thesis is summarized in Figure 3.7 below.

A long-standing assumption in the field of strategic management is that strategy is "equifinal," meaning that there are many strategic paths that can be followed to the same end, and that no path is inherently superior to others. Figure 3.7 challenges this assumption. It shows that there are certain strategic paths a company *must* follow, and that these paths are determined by the type of business model the company employs. The path a company must follow is not a matter of free choice but rather a consequence of decisions made at the company's inception, as described in Chapter 2. Think of it as a corollary to the old nature vs. nurture debate: model-creating decisions are permanent, immutable strategic influences and their influence must always be considered.

Thus, this chapter's core thesis—that business model type influences the competitive strategies that are pursued—is a radical notion. And the implication of this notion is radical as well: if your company's competitive strategies don't pursue the described customer pool management objectives, they should.

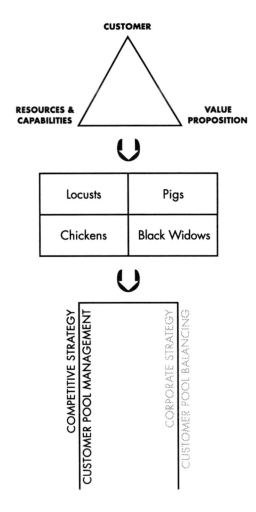

FIGURE 3.7   SUMMARY OF CHAPTER 3

I don't mean to identify here all the means to pursue those objectives. Indeed, the examples I've provided merely scratch the surface of how they could be pursued. Failure to pursue the customer pool objectives defined by your business model, though, is a sure path to strategic confusion and under-performance.

In this chapter I've limited the narrative strictly to the way a type of business model influences those competitive strategies *related specifically to it*. In other words, I focused each type of business model under a lens and said, "For this model type, we see that these are the related issues and competitive strategy practices that should be pursued." I used this pedagogical device as a means of explaining the related points as simply, clearly, and concisely as possible.

In practice, most companies employ more than one business model type and hence have multiple customer pools. Customer pools are generally managed (a) as individual entities (as discussed in this chapter) and (b) as elements of what Figure 3.7 identifies as the *corporate customer pool*. Let's turn our attention now to the more complex issue of managing the corporate customer pool.

4

Corporate Strategy

Few enterprises are as simple as those described in the preceding chapter. Most are active in multiple markets and have multiple revenue streams. These companies are *diversified*.

In business model terms, a diversified corporation is composed of different types of business models. *Corporate* strategy is concerned with the design and management of the total set of business models. Corporate strategy decides which business models belong in the enterprise and how they should be connected to one another.

MULTI-BUSINESS ENTERPRISES

Why would management decide to add more businesses to the enterprise? As shown in the previous chapter, managing a business's customer pool is a complex, long-term task. Why would a top executive choose to make matters more complex by adding a new business, and hence another customer pool requiring management, into the corporate mix? Here are two reasons.

First, management may have no choice. Technological change can upset or make obsolete even the most effective business model. Kodak (NYSE: EK), for example, has watched its traditional business (silver halide photographic film) go into a free fall in the face of digital imaging technology. In search of a viable business model to replace the now obsolete one, Kodak has added many new businesses:

- Digital labs and kiosks, both aimed at securing image-printing revenues from locations where these facilities are in place
- Hardware (digital cameras and printers)
- Internet sites where consumers can store and display their digital photos.

Second, and most significant, diversification is a principal means by which a company can overcome the structural disadvantage inherent in its core business's model type (see Chapter 3). A Black Widow business, for example, can only break out of its dependence upon its key customer(s) by diversifying. As we saw in Chapter 1, Boots and Coots turned to diversification when it confronted an intractable Response (Pig) business. Locust businesses diversify as a means of enhancing or extending their value propositions and drawing back lost customers.

Diversification

While the principles of business-model–based diversification are fully scalable, applying equally to both small and large businesses, it's easiest to see and understand them by looking at small enterprises.

At first glance, a neighborhood florist seems to be strategically uninteresting. The business is small, often consisting of an owner, a handful of employees, and a small storefront. The florist's product and service mix is essentially the same as that of its rivals. Location is therefore a primary means by which florists differentiate themselves.

On closer examination, though, we see that the florist business is in fact strategically complex and subtle. It is, potentially, an enterprise of three separate business models:

1. *Locust business.* Retail clients access the florist either by walking into the store, phoning in orders, or via the Internet.
2. *Pig business.* The florist provides flower arrangements, apparel complements, and decorative items for events such as weddings and bar mitzvahs.
3. *Chicken business.* The florist provides floral arrangements to local institutions (churches, hotels, restaurants, etc.) on a pre-scheduled basis.

Figure 4.1 below diagrams the florist's portfolio of businesses. The florist, a small business, is diversified: it comprises more than one business model type.

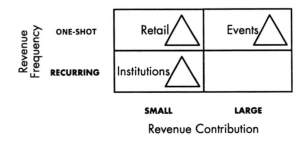

FIGURE 4.1   A DIVERSIFIED FLORIST

Compound Businesses

In 1995, Jeff Bezos founded Amazon.com (NASDAQ: AMZN) as "the world's biggest bookstore." In 1998 Bezos added music and movies to the Internet retailer's product mix, along with product categories including cameras, houseware, and lawn furniture.

But adding these product categories did not *diversify* Amazon.com, at least from a business model perspective. Amazon.com started as a Locust business, and every one of its new products either extended the preexisting Locust business or created a new Locust business. The new products did not add a Chicken, Pig, or Black Widow business to Amazon.com; therefore, they did *not* diversify the company.[6]

The same can be said of Wal-Mart's move into groceries. Wal-Mart's retail arm is a Locust business. The grocery business, added in the mid-1990s, is another Locust business. Thus, Wal-Mart is *not* diversified.

Amazon.com and Wal-Mart are *compound businesses,* corporations comprising multiple business models of the same type. Both companies created new businesses by leveraging preexisting resources and capabilities; in both companies, resources are shared between the separate business models. For example, all of Amazon.com's product extensions are shipped through the company's state-of-the-art fulfillment centers; Wal-Mart moves everything it sells (from clothing to canned beets) through its inventory receiving system.

In general, companies that leverage their resources and capabilities to create new businesses tend to build compound enterprises. Given the Chapter 2 discussion of the separate resource orientations of each business model type, this makes sense; it's logical that they would spawn businesses designed to offer similar types of solutions to their customers.

Corporate Customer Pools

The previous chapters introduced the concept of the customer pool as a company's active customers. Extending that discussion, we can distinguish two different types of customer pools:

---

[6]Note that, from a business model perspective, Amazon.com *did* diversify in 2000, when the company started providing order-fulfillment services to other online retailers. Its first customer, signed to a multi-year contract, was Toys 'R Us. Order fulfillment was, and is, a Chicken business. Diversifying into this Chicken business (and acquiring additional order-fulfillment customers) is the main reason why Amazon.com is now profitable.

1. The total number of active customers associated with a particular business model, or the *business model customer pool*
2. The total number of active customers served by the enterprise, or the *corporate customer pool*

To simplify the discussion, let A represent the business model customer pool and B the corporate customer pool.

In the case of a *single-business enterprise,* {A = B}. In other words, a single-business enterprise's business model customer pool is equivalent to the corporate customer pool.

In the case of a *compound or diversified enterprise,* the company comprises more than one business model; therefore, $B = \{A_1, A_2 \dots A_n\}$. In other words, the corporate customer pool of an enterprise comprising multiple business models is the set of all the different business model customer pools the corporation owns.

Figure 4.2 below contrasts the customer pools of the three corporate forms (single business, compound, and diversified). Note the following:

1. For the *single-business enterprise,* A = B. The business model customer pool is identical to the corporate customer pool.
2. For the *compound enterprise,* $B = \{A_1, A_2\}$. The corporate customer pool comprises two separate business model pools, A_1 and A_2. The corporate customer pool is *homogeneous* in that all the customers are alike (in this case, Locusts).
3. For the *diversified enterprise,* $\{B = A_3, A_4\}$. The corporate customer pool comprises two business model pools, A_3 and A_4. The corporate customer pool is *heterogeneous* in that it includes customers of different types (in this case, Chickens and Pigs).

Figure 4.2 does not include all corporate forms. A complex entity that could be classified both compound and diversified is shown below in

SINGLE BUSINESS COMPOUND DIVERSIFIED

FIGURE 4.2 CORPORATE CUSTOMER POOLS

Figure 4.3. This form is generally seen only in the largest corporations. We'll discuss this complex form at the end of the chapter.

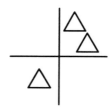

FIGURE 4.3 COMPLEX CORPORATE CUSTOMER POOL

PORTFOLIO DESIGN

The term "portfolio" is used in corporate strategy to describe the business units that constitute the corporation. In business model terms, portfolio refers to the business model pools $\{A_n\}$ that make up the corporate customer pool: $B = \{A_1, A_2, A_3, \dots A_n\}$.

The presence of any business model within the corporate customer pool $\{B\}$ is a matter of management choice, the outcome of executive-level management's decision to be in Business A_1, Business A_2, etc. While it's possible that management could make separate decisions regarding each business ("Should we be in Business A_n?"), a more considered and practical approach would be to make such a decision by including {B} as a factor. In other words, the decision to be in Business A_n should consider whether and how A_n "fits" within {B}.

The criteria that determine this "fit" are discussed below.

Customer Sharing

Chapter 1 described the diversification of Boots and Coots. In 2004, the company was composed of two business model types, a Chicken business (Prevention) and a Pig business (Response). The two business models did not have separate customer pools; they *shared customers.*

In the event of an accident, a Prevention customer would almost certainly become a Response customer. Likewise, a Response customer would presumably find the value proposition of Boots and Coots' Prevention business compelling as a means of reducing the likelihood of future accidents. Under certain circumstances, a customer might belong to both customer pools at the same time. Figure 4.4 illustrates customer sharing.

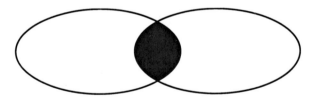

FIGURE 4.4   CUSTOMER SHARING

Many other combinations of business models share clients. Consider, for example, the industry that designs and installs fire-suppression systems found in restaurant kitchens. The industry will be home to two separate business models:

Chickens & Pigs

1. Sophisticated and expensive engineering is needed to design and install a system that is complex, customized to the customer's specific situation. This is a classic Pig business.
2. Legal and insurance requirements require that such systems be inspected and maintained regularly. This is a Chicken business.

The company that diversifies—that makes itself capable of both designing and installing and maintaining the systems—is in a position to retain the Pig customer that would otherwise be lost once installation is complete. Diversification lets the installer transform the Pig customer into a Chicken customer.

As suggested by this example, diversification that produces customer sharing is associated with industries in which complex systems are designed and installed and then maintained (for example, heating and ventilation units, turbine generators). Note that maintenance can take different forms, ranging from on-site inspections to the sale of replacement parts.

Customer Pool Balancing

Most business commentators suggest that the formation of compound enterprises is ideal for companies seeking to become multi-business corporations. Two reasons are typically cited:
1. Because of the similarity between the separately owned business models, management is said to know and understand how to operate the businesses.
2. The shared resources that often produce compound businesses also yield operating efficiencies.

From a business model perspective, however, compounding is a poor option. In principle, compounding magnifies corporate exposure to the structural inadequacies of a given type of business model. For example, a corporation consisting of two Locust businesses must manage two businesses, each of which is subject to losing customers; an enterprise composed of two Pig businesses must manage two widely varying customer pools; a company composed of two Black Widow businesses must suffer "dependency squared."

In contrast to compounding, diversification offers the opportunity to balance and compensate for the structural inadequacies of other owned business models:

- Locust businesses and Pig businesses lose their customers. Diversification can "catch" these customers and retain them elsewhere in the enterprise.

- Pig businesses have very unstable customer pools. Diversification can provide a base of stable revenues that allows the Pig business to survive the dry spells.

- Black Widow businesses depend upon powerful customers. Diversification can break that dependency and create a vibrant business that excludes the all-powerful customer.

Diversification vs. Compounding

The argument in favor of diversification over compounding is radical. Most commentators use the term "related diversification" to describe what they see as diversification that has the highest likelihood of success. They see such relatedness in enterprises that are, from a business model perspective, compound entities. They point to companies like Wal-Mart as exemplars of the related diversification approach. I suggest that closer analysis reveals flaws in the view that compound enterprises are somehow superior.

Nobody can argue with the success of Wal-Mart's move into groceries. From a standing start, they've become America's largest grocery business. More significantly, the two business models also appear to share customers. Indeed, one of the reasons Wal-Mart decided to add groceries to its retail mix was that they believed each business would draw customers to the other.

On close examination, though, we see that Wal-Mart's customer sharing differs from the customer-sharing examples discussed above. Wal-Mart's customers are not retained by either model. The retailer only achieves temporary customer sharing. Once the transactions are completed, the customer is gone. Adding a Locust business has not changed Wal-Mart's corporate customer pool: the company's customers are all Locusts. It has not compensated for structural limitations of the core Locust business.

Worse still, the creation of the Wal-Mart super center has introduced problems related to slow checkout and difficult customer parking. A business model perspective on these problems suggests that they are more than mere operational concerns. Rather, they strike at the heart of how a Locust business succeeds: by making things easy for customers. Any benefits from Wal-Mart's compounding will disappear once the retail giant has transformed all its stores to super centers.

Find the Chicken

Diversification can move in any direction: a Pig business can create a Black Widow business, a Locust business can buy a Pig business, a Chicken business can create a Locust business, and so on. In general, however, diversification should strive to add a Chicken business for these reasons:

1. *Chicken businesses are appealing because of their potential to generate the highest gross and net profit margins.* Their stable revenue

streams can also be leveraged to support bold new ventures. These same revenue streams are a potential haven should such ventures fail.

2. *Chicken businesses are valuable for corporate customer pool management.* Customer sharing works best when the lost customer (a Locust or a Pig) becomes a Chicken (a customer who is retained over successive time periods).

All else being equal, the goal for businesses to "Find the Chicken" should underlie all their diversification activities. Indeed, "Find the Chicken" is a good mantra for any company seeking to free itself from the limitations and problems of its existing (presumably non-Chicken) businesses.

Consider the turnaround that International Business Machines (NYSE: IBM) accomplished in the 1990s. The company's finances reached a low point in 1992 when it lost $5 billion, prompting *The Economist* to recommend breaking up Big Blue. By the end of the decade, however, CEO Louis Gerstner had transformed IBM into a company known for the services it provided rather than the hardware it manufactured. A critical component in that turnaround was a series of long-term (Chicken) contracts IBM signed with major customers who hired IBM to manage everything from their e-commerce web sites to their entire IT operation. By early 1999, IBM had booked $51 billion in these Chicken contracts.

The benefits of adding Chickens to an existing portfolio aren't limited to high-technology industries, nor are they beneficial only to companies in urgent need of a turnaround. In 1994, General Electric (NYSE: GE) announced a major initiative that continues today—a push to find *product services*. One example of GE's product service efforts is the company's medical business placing diagnostic sensors and communications capabilities into their installed base of CT scanners and MRI equipment. Called "In Site," the devices allowed continuous diagnosis of the devices' operating conditions. Customers pay for the monitoring, making the business a Chicken. This In Site idea was then shared with other GE businesses. Recognizing how much customers would value such information, the company's jet engine business, in particular, eagerly embraced a program for monitoring engines while they were in flight.

These examples from GM and IBM are but two of dozens that I could use to illustrate the fundamental value of "Finding the Chicken": *any business model that competes with a structural disadvantage will benefit from adding a Chicken business.*

For example, Intuit (NASDAQ: INTU), the software company that writes and sells Quicken, QuickBooks, and TurboTax, struggled financially for many years. The Locust business lost an average of $34 million each year from 1992 through 1998. In 1998, Intuit created a Chicken business that shared a Locust customer by offering itself as an outsource payroll solution provider for small businesses using QuickBooks. The impact was significant and almost immediate: Intuit averaged an 18.6 percent net earnings margin each year from 1999 through 2004.

Hewitt Associates (NYSE: HEW) is a large Pig business, a $2.3 billion human resource consulting company that added a Chicken business in 1991 when it started administering 401K plans for a small group of its roughly 2,500 clients. By 1999, the Chicken had grown to represent about 65 percent of the company's sales, and the number of total participants had grown to 18 million. More impressive still was the earnings performance of Hewitt's newly created Chicken business. From 1999 to 2004, 401K outsourcing revenues grew at a compound annual rate of 25 percent. Over the same period, gross margins in this line of business grew at the rate of 6 percent. These results contrast sharply with the performance of Hewitt's core consulting (Pig) business. Over the same period (1999 through 2004), gross margins collapsed, shrinking a total of 54 percent, while operating income declined 19 percent. In 2002, Hewitt went public with the expressly stated aim of building its Chicken business through acquisitions.

"Finding the Chicken" is relatively difficult for the Black Widow business because customer sharing is not an option that can be pursued. They must diversify by building a Chicken business from scratch. The process is costly, time consuming, and uncertain.

Delphi (Pink Sheets: DPHIQ) diversified by leveraging the skills of engineers to create a range of new products, including sophisticated motion sensors found in everything from state-of-the-art wheelchairs to the much-hyped Segway scooter, and key components used by satellite radio rivals Sirius (NASDAQ: SIRI) and XM (NASDAQ: XMSR). Neither of these ventures was clearly a Chicken business when Delphi slipped into Chapter 11 bankruptcy protection, but the company's diversification ventures are notable because former-parent General Motors (NYSE: GM) was not a client. Indeed, Delphi had been so successful at reducing its dependence upon GM that it removed the term "automotive" from its name. By 2004, 50 percent of Delphi's sales were to non-GM customers.[7]

A DOSE OF REALITY

A word of caution: Before you go off and diversify wildly, pointing to this volume as your justification, consider the following: Strategic

---

[7]Delphi's Chapter 11 status was largely the result of labor-related costs it inherited when it was spun off from GM. The company's insolvency had nothing to do with diversification into new businesses.

management researchers have amassed a library of empirical studies all pointing in the same direction: more often than not, diversification *loses* value for both the company and its shareholders. Thus, academics tend to frown upon diversification as a strategy. They counsel that if diversification is something top managers want to pursue (despite the preponderance of evidence against it), they should not stray too far from their core business and "proceed with caution."

In this light, the C&P argument in favor of diversification (and against compounding) appears radical. Viewed more closely, though, only one type of corporate diversification "move" is recommended: *diversify to find the Chicken.* From the perspective of designing a corporate customer pool, finding the Chicken holds the greatest potential for success.

Also be aware that *thinking* you're adding a Chicken business to your corporate portfolio doesn't necessarily mean you're actually doing so. To see what I mean, consider the cautionary tale of Newell Rubbermaid (NYSE: NWL).

Few acquisitions have proved as disastrous as Newell's 1998 purchase of Rubbermaid. In the 10 years before the Rubbermaid deal, Newell's shareholders enjoyed average annual returns of 23 percent, four points ahead of the S&P 500 index. The total market value of the two companies at the time of the acquisition was $12 billion. By the end of 2004, the merged company was worth less than half that. The stock price peaked at $50 in 1999; in 2004, it dipped below $20.

The outcome of the Rubbermaid acquisition is noteworthy in part because of Newell's high stature prior to the purchase. They had become a centerpiece of MBA instruction, hailed as a company with a resource-based *competitive* advantage and a resource-based *corporate* advantage. Newell was a company in which observers saw manufacturing, merchandising, and marketing capabilities so strong that the company was considered a paragon of the "parenting advantage" concept. In fact, Newell was so experienced at buying and turning around acquisitions that its turnaround process ("Newellization") itself was praised as a competence.

Newell, Pre-Rubbermaid

Newell identified its product-market direction in 1967, formally stating its intention to focus on hardware and do-it-yourself products sold to volume retailers. Future customers would include Wal-Mart, Target, Staples, and Home Depot. Over the next 20 years, the company acquired more than 30 major businesses, building full-ranged product lines in product areas like draperies (including hardware, blinds, and shades), hardware products (e.g., paint brushes), writing instruments, and cookware. Their brands included Levelor, Kirsch, Sanford, Sharpie, Anchor Hocking, Pyrex, Mirror, and WearEver.

From their customers' perspective, Newell made and sold items that were "must-haves," items retailers believed they had to have on hand for customers. Each item took up floor space, and retailers wanted these must-haves to generate as many dollars per square foot (sales revenue, earnings) as possible.

Newell had become expert at managing ongoing customer problems. To ensure product was always on hand when its customers came looking for these items, Newell made itself the gold-standard for line-fill (the measure of stock available when the retailer received a shipment) and on-time delivery. To maximize the generated amount of dollars per square foot of floor space, Newell set up and actively managed the in-store displays of its products in three categories ("good," "better," and "best"). By carefully selecting the attributes that defined the categories and engineering the displays to highlight these differences, customers were always encouraged to purchase a higher-priced, higher-margin version of the product.

Framed in the terms of this chapter, Newell was a compound business operating a series of Chicken businesses. Although not contractually bound to its customers, Newell enjoyed recurring transactions with each. It managed product categories its customers needed to maintain, and it generated high returns for each square foot allocated to those displays.

The 1998 Rubbermaid Acquisition

The $6 billion Rubbermaid acquisition price was steep, and some raised concerns about Newell's capacity to turn around so large an acquisition. But the general reaction of those few who were paying attention was that Rubbermaid and Newell fit together well. Three factors made Rubbermaid attractive to Newell:

1. *The two companies sold to the same customer* (Wal-Mart was Rubbermaid's biggest customer).
2. *The two companies sold houseware* (at 46 percent of sales, houseware constituted Rubbermaid's largest product line).
3. *Rubbermaid was experiencing severe problems with on-time shipments and inventory replenishment,* two operational areas in which Newell excelled and which "Newellization" directly addressed.

From a business model perspective, though, Newell underestimated the significance of certain elements related to Rubbermaid's business:

1. *The company generated sales through product innovation.* In 1994 alone, the company launched over 400 new products. A third of Rubbermaid's 1994 sales came from products introduced in the five preceding years.

2. *Rubbermaid relied heavily upon brand to drive sales.* In the early 1990s, *Fortune* magazine named the company "America's Most Admired Firm" two years in a row.

3. *Rubbermaid's value proposition was not built around "must-have" items.* Retailers had more discretion in whether or not to carry the items and in the levels of inventory. Retailers were also more price-sensitive in these product areas. When plastic resin prices rose in early 1994, Rubbermaid had been unable to pass along the increased raw material costs to retailers.

4. *Rubbermaid's 10K filings to the SEC indicated heavy reliance (roughly 15 percent of annual sales) upon an unnamed retailer (likely Wal-Mart).* While not clearly a Black Widow business, Rubbermaid certainly had a customer upon whom it depended heavily and whose loss would be painful.

5. *The company's filings did not indicate that it managed a problem for its customers.* Rubbermaid defined itself as a plastics manufacturer. There was no section of Wal-Mart (or any discount retailer) that Rubbermaid could claim as its own.

When Newell purchased Rubbermaid, they thought they were buying a Chicken business. In reality, Newell bought a Locust business. Worse, Newell bought an unhealthy Locust business, given Rubbermaid's dependence on Wal-Mart.

The purchase of a Locust business diversified Newell (a compound business made up of Chicken businesses prior to this purchase). The results have been devastating, as shown below in Table 4.1

TABLE 4.1 NEWELL RUBBERMAIDS' FINANCES

YEAR (DECEMBER)	REVENUE ($ MILLION)	NET INCOME ($ MILLION)	NET PROFIT MARGIN (%)
2004	6,748.4	(116.1)	–
2003	7,750.0	(46.6)	–
2002	7,453.9	(203.4)	–
2001	6,909.3	264.6	3.8
2000	6,934.7	421.6	6.1
1999	6,413.1	95.4	1.5
1998	3,720.0	396.2	10.7
1997	3,234.3	290.4	9.0
1996	2,872.8	256.5	8.9
1995	2,498.4	222.5	8.9
1994	2,074.9	195.6	9.4

Source: www.hoovers.com

Now we can see why no one has carte blanche to diversify whenever one of their businesses proves difficult to manage. The message of Newell is that diversification should be in one direction only (Find the Chicken) and always pursued with caution.

LOOSE ENDS

Two topics, one implicit and one previously noted, merit closer examination before we end this chapter.

Corporate Strategy and the Chicken Business

This chapter's discussion of diversification was in large part directed at non-Chicken businesses. But what about Chicken businesses themselves? Should they diversify? Does "Find the Chicken" apply to them, too?

The "Find the Chicken" directive is more than the central theme of this chapter: it is, to a large extent, the message of this entire book. Even though following this dictate would, in the case of a Chicken business, mean compounding its corporate customer pool, the "Find the Chicken" message is as valid for the Chicken business as for any other type of business model.

A more substantive question is: under what circumstances will compounding make sense for a Chicken business? What would push an inherently conservative company, one anxious to protect its core business, to make its corporate customer pool more complex by adding another business model to it? Three factors stand out:

1. *Shareholder pressure to grow rapidly plagues a large number of publicly traded companies.* Given its inherent need to grow slowly and carefully, the Chicken business's model is particularly vulnerable under such pressure. Newell's acquisition of Rubbermaid can be attributed in large part to this growth demand.

2. *Consolidation within the customer industry can jeopardize even a robust Chicken business.* Adding a new Chicken business represents a means of avoiding the Black Widow trap.

3. *Competitive pressures may force a Chicken business to update its value proposition.* Customer sharing between two Chicken business models would not repair the defect in one or the other model, but it would retain customers who might otherwise be lost.

Complex Corporations

In an earlier part of this chapter, we noted that some corporations have corporate customer pools that could be categorized as both diversified and compound (refer again to Figure 4.3). How should we assess such a corporation?

Conglomerates, even in the entertainment industry, are an unpopular organizational form today; it's unlikely that any business not currently resembling Figure 4.3 will ever assume this type of complexity. Our analysis should therefore be directed at those organizations that currently have this "unclassifiable portfolio" and are facing pressures, both internally and from shareholders, to divest all but their "core" businesses.

Organizational restructuring has become something of a managerial art. Businesses are grouped together across criteria that include product, geography, and, on occasion, customers. I would suggest that customer pool issues are a powerful set of criteria for restructuring. Divisions can be created on the basis of

- customer pools that share customers;
- customer pools of compound business models; and
- unconnected business models.

This type of restructuring would do more than simply rearrange the business pieces. Poorly constructed or unconnected corporate customer pools would jump out as likely candidates for divestiture. Conversely, customer pools that share customers and have a Chicken business as their foundation would emerge as entities to be retained.

SUMMARY

Most contemporary business strategists speak of building an organization's "competencies," and when they speak of corporate strategy, they take that logic with them. Theirs is an advocacy of "corporate advantage," the concept that a business should be enhanced competitively by being part of the corporate whole. Organizations that share or transfer competencies, their thinking goes, are likely to generate this type of advantage.

The relationship between this chapter's concepts and those discussed in Chapters 2 and 3 supports the coherence, if not the specifics, of these contemporary business strategists. As shown below in Figure 4.5, the essence of the C&P framework—the element that unifies the different branches of strategy and provides substance to both analysis and prescription—is the customer pool.

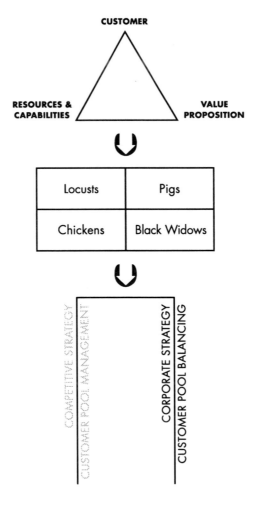

FIGURE 4.5   SUMMARY OF CHAPTER 4

I don't see the role of corporate strategy as that of enhancing the competitive effectiveness of each owned business model. A business model exists on its own. The limitations of each type of business model are structural and cannot be made to disappear.

The role of corporate strategy is to build an enterprise from business models with flawed parts. If the strategy is well crafted, the resulting entity will be one in which one business model *balances* and *compensates* for the customer pool weaknesses of another. A balanced entity's corporate customer pool holds customers that individual business models would otherwise lose. Retained customers are kept active by "cross-selling" them the products and services of different corporate-owned business models. This is the essence of *corporate synergy.*[8]

---

[8]Refer to the Introduction to see how the customer pool approach to synergy contrasts with synergy as traditionally defined and pursued.

5
Synthesis

We've covered a lot of ground and in considerable detail. You may be feeling a bit overwhelmed. Before we go on to discuss how you can apply the ideas presented in the previous chapters, let's summarize the main points covered thus far.

BUSINESS MODELS

- Every business possesses at least one model.
- Business models describe revenue streams. These streams are categorized by the scale of a customer's contribution to total revenues and the frequency with which these contributions are made.
- Business models are created by three closely related decisions: the customer to be served, the value proposition to be offered to the customer, and the resources and capabilities that will create and/or deliver the value proposition. Business models are permanent. Once created, they cannot be altered.
- Four busines model types exist, each associated with a different type of cash flow, a distinct relationship with its customers, and a unique customer pool.

- Business models are constructed to resolve customer problems. Each type of business model offers a different type of solution.
- Companies organize themselves internally to deliver the different types of solutions. These different internal resource arrangements explain why business model types are permanent and why one type of model type cannot easily offer solutions that another type of model can offer.

STRATEGIES

- The competitive and corporate strategies a company pursues should be determined by the type of business model.
- Competitive strategies manage model-specific customer pools. These strategies center on (a) customer acquisition, (b) customer retention, and (c) customer reacquisition. Different types of business models have different abilities and limitations with respect to each customer pool management task.
- Corporate strategies engineer the composition of the corporate customer pool. Adding a Chicken business that shares customers with a preexisting business model offers the potential to retain customers and cross-sell to them, thereby stabilizing revenues and earnings.

GENERAL THEMES

- *Find the Chicken.* There is no more effective way to tame an otherwise uncontrollable enterprise. You've met your goal when Chicken business revenues constitute from 30 to 50 percent of total corporate sales.

- *Hold onto Your Customers.* Keep them out of the market and in your customer pool. If your business model doesn't allow you to do this directly, use corporate strategy to create a corporate customer pool that achieves this end.

6

Implementation

As outlined in the Introduction, "strategy" has a perceptual dimension. Most strategy objects are cognitive; what you see is largely a matter of what you look for. As shown in Table 6.1, C&P offers a different way of looking at strategy. Along with this new view comes the possibility of developing entirely new objectives and using a range of new and distinct diagnostic tools.

TABLE 6.1 STRATEGIC MANAGEMENT PARADIGMS

	CLASSIC (PORTER)	CONTEMPORARY (RBV)	CHICKENS & PIGS
Mode	Plan	Learn	Listen
Objective	Find a sustainable position	Build a sustainable competitive advantage	Retain customers
Tools	Industry analysis Market segmentation	Core competencies Knowledge	Business models Customer pools
Key resource	Capital	Capabilities	Customers

The approaches to strategy diagrammed in Table 6.1 are not either-or considerations. Each approach focuses on different aspects of the strategy-making challenge. To adopt a C&P orientation to your strategic management activities, you won't have to abandon your assessments of the industry in which you compete or jettison the work you've put into identifying and developing your competencies.

C&P is a customer-centered approach to strategy development; this is what makes C&P stand out in contrast to more widely used strategic management frameworks. Making C&P part of your strategic thinking will make the customer the center of your strategic endeavors; this will result in a new set of priorities for your strategic tools and pursuits.

GETTING STARTED

Before you can go forward with C&P, you have to know where you stand now. The first step is to analyze the current business (or businesses) you operate. Do you own a Chicken business? What are the business models that constitute your corporate customer pool? What proportion of your total revenues and earnings does each of your owned business models contribute?

The challenge presented by this first step is formidable. As suggested in Chapter 2, a deep understanding of your business model(s) begins with an examination of them in terms of the Transaction Frequency and Revenue Contribution axes shown in Figure 1.1. Your business may well have model aspects that point in different directions. Locust businesses often have repeat customers; many Chicken businesses have customers that represent a disproportionate share of revenues. You are likely to discover a similar mix of contradictory signals when you look at the model(s) you own. Judgment will play a part in how you classify your efforts.

In addition, internal obstacles may rear up and make the task of classifying your business model difficult:

1. *Some managers may not accept the classification(s).* C&P has a hierarchy in which one business model type is "best." Managers may want their units to be classified as Chickens, believing such a classification will earn them status and internal rewards.

2. *The data required for analyzing your business-model portfolio may not be readily available.* As you try to find hard data to help you categorize your businesses, you may run into problems. First, you may have no customer-level data to analyze. Managers have not been trained to collect and use customer-level data. Second, you may not have the kind of financial data that will allow you to generate performance profiles for each of your business models.

Your financial information may be based upon lump-sum revenues. These issues are not fatal. They just mean you will have to start using C&P with rough assessments based upon your instincts and those of any other managers you bring into the process. If you don't now have data that will allow you to analyze your customer pools systematically, modify your internal systems to begin generating such data. Then review your initial business-model assessments later, when you have data to buttress the classification process.

C&P requires you to monitor the shape and performance of each model's customer pool regularly. Example metrics you will likely want to develop and track over time include

- the size of (number of customers in) each business model's customer pool;
- the rate of period-to-period customer-pool growth;
- the period-to-period net leakage percentage;
- the time a customer remains in the pool;

- the acquisition and reacquisition cost per new customer; and
- revenues and earnings per customer.

If your enterprise comprises multiple business models, you will also need to measure the revenue and profitability contributions made by each model to the corporate whole.

In general, the more historical strategic data you are able to gather, the more you will learn about what has (and has not) worked. If this information is too hard to collect or is simply unavailable, start generating this type of data going forward. As you'll see below, the only way you can fairly assess how well you're doing is by analyzing high-quality, internally generated data.

REFINE YOUR VALUE PROPOSITION

Many executives buy into the idea that strategy is rooted internally, in a company's resources and capabilities. "What you're capable of doing is what you should do," goes the argument. "If you stick to your core business, you'll find a pot of gold waiting for you," is the message of the viewpoint's most passionate advocates.

Wrong.

As anybody who has ever started or developed a business knows, the customer comes first. *Without the customer, there is no business.*

You don't win a customer with your resources and capabilities. You win the customer with the value proposition you offer him or her. If you have special resources and capabilities that let you offer the customer something that your rivals can't offer or imitate, great; if this means you can charge a ridiculously high price for your value proposition, better still. If your resources and capabilities are truly unique, that's the best possible value proposition to have. And a compelling value proposition wins the customer.

C&P says that you cannot simply leverage existing resources and capabilities to create a value proposition you like or are able to deliver. Your opinion isn't the one that counts, and your capabilities neither determine nor define the customer's requirements. Your *customer's* opinion is the only one that counts. That customer must find your value proposition compelling.

From this point forward, stop thinking of strategy in terms of what you *can* do (your resources and capabilities). Start thinking about what you *must* do to offer and deliver a compelling value proposition to your customer. In other words, frame your resource requirements in terms of your value proposition.

If you lack the resources and capabilities that allow you to develop a compelling value proposition, you must do one of two things:

1. Acquire them (e.g., by hiring or by acquiring a company that possesses the needed capabilities).
2. Gain temporary or indirect access to them, either by outsourcing to a specialist that possesses them or by entering into a joint venture or partnership with a company that has them.

The product or service you offer is unquestionably a part of that value proposition. As we'll see in the next section, however, a compelling value proposition involves key intangibles, too. To identify and recognize these, you must see things from the customer's viewpoint.

GAINING A CUSTOMER'S-EYE VIEW

You may see the role of your business as meeting customer needs. The needs-based perspective is part of today's prevailing management paradigm.

Needs are related to individuals' motivations and perceptions, and a needs-based perspective is effective as a basis for understanding why an individual consumer may prefer one brand over another. While this perspective can provide critical information for marketing programs aimed at persuading individual consumers to purchase certain products or services, it becomes strained when the customer is another business.

Theorists array an individual's needs hierarchically, from lower-level "subsistence" needs to higher-level needs like "growth" and "self-actualization." A person's behaviors and motivations are said to be driven by the level of need being pursued. But business organizations don't have higher-level needs. While they depend upon resources for survival, businesses do not bring human needs such as growth or self-actualization into the equation.

C&P does not take a needs-based view of the company. Instead C&P recognizes that all customers, whether individuals or organizations, have problems. The company with a customer's-eye view sees these problems and perceives them as potential paths to a compelling value proposition.

In general, customer problems offer two types of value-proposition opportunities:

1. *Differentiation opportunities* exist in settings where customer problems are either wholly unaddressed by rivals or addressed poorly or incompletely.
2. *Cost/efficiency opportunities* exist in settings where rivals address customer problems inefficiently and hence charge higher-than-necessary prices for the solutions they offer.

Customer problems can be found even in settings where a needs-based orientation prevails. Locust businesses, for example, sell directly to individuals. These businesses are those that tend to find great value in thinking in terms of customer needs. But consider the recent success retail giant Wal-Mart has enjoyed with its super centers. While they offer customers great savings, these super centers have inadvertently presented customers with two *new* problems: crowded parking lots and long checkout lines. Rivals could capitalize on these problems by offering customers problem-free alternatives.

The Wal-Mart example points to two themes that can help a company seeking to develop compelling value propositions: (a) customer problems can arise as a side effect of satisfying the customer's needs and (b) customer problems can relate to customer emotions, most notably fear and/or frustration. A company that wants to tap into these fears and frustrations in order to create a value proposition can do so by asking the customer two questions: *What problem keeps you awake at night? How can we help you solve it?*

CUSTOMER POOL MANAGEMENT

Strategies to manage customer pools can take two forms:

1. *Model maximization* aims to increase the size and profitability of the business-level customer pools.
2. *Model balancing* strives to create a corporate customer pool that contains a Chicken component.

The two are not mutually exclusive; you can choose to pursue one, the other, or both.

Business Model Maximization

Most executives think of business maximization in financial terms—sales or profits. We saw in Chapter 2 that gross and net earnings rely heavily on business model type. Consider how pricing, for example, is influenced by model type:

1. Business models that retain customers from period to period (such as Chickens or Black Widows) are, all things being equal, much more willing to sacrifice short-term profitability if it means retaining the customer. Such compromises can extend for multiple time periods.

2. Business models that lose their customers (such as Locusts or Pigs) are interested in short-term profit performance—that is, returns from those customers the company is doing business with in the current time period. The charged price is typically as high as the market will bear, and fiercely applied cost controls (and cost-cutting when needed) are applied to drive up short-term profitability.

Rather than use financial outcomes as a business's score card, I believe that business model maximization is best measured in customer terms. Further, I believe the core objective of business model maximization is to increase the number of customers within the pool without compromising delivery of the value proposition. In order to maximize the latent financial potential within a business model, customers must be acquired.

In general, business model maximization is achieved by developing strategies to engineer and control customer pool inflows and outflows. Each pool has its own "dominant logic"—the pool-management challenge related to its inherent customer-flow patterns. Table 6.2 summarizes model-specific differences.

Tactical Themes

To accumulate customers, Chicken businesses need to make credible promises to potential customers. They need to be able to point to current customers as recommendation sources. For Chicken businesses, customer acquisition and prevention of customer loss are facilitated

TABLE 6.2 IMPLEMENTING CHICKENS & PIGS

	CHICKEN	PIG	LOCUST	BLACK WIDOW
Customer Pool Growth Tendencies				
Dominant Logic	Accumulate annuity-like customers.	Smooth out peaks and troughs.	Replace lost customers.	Prevent customer loss.
Customer Pool Management Goals	Accumulate customers organically through market activities. Acquire customers through horizontal integration.	Build client competencies Secure long-lived, multi-year projects.	Find new customers through physical growth. Win back old customers.	Deepen ties with customers through multiple programs.
Establish (Tactics; Actions)	"Promise credibility"; achieve through •quality programs •focus on process (standardization)	Reputation; sole (or only "real") RFQ invitee	Brand; achieve through consistency in •innovation (R&D) •marketing	Efficiency (delivered value divided by cost); achieve through •process improvements, excellence •develop value proposition to solve more customer problems

by making *quality* a central part of their strategy. Regardless of the quality assurance program adopted (ISO; Six Sigma; TQM; etc.), the focus of that program must be the elimination of process variance from all internal operations that affect the value proposition delivered to customers. Current customers must be served perfectly.

Pig businesses typically win customers by bidding for projects. A Pig business wants to either be the only bidder or, in the case of competitive bids, the only serious contender. To achieve this position, a Pig business must establish itself as the expert in its field, the *authority* whose participation in a project provides immediate assurance the job is in good hands. Employees, including the key managers, must publish articles in respected periodicals and journals. Executives must become publicly active in government projects and community programs. Publicizing these activities for maximum effect must be done professionally.

Locust businesses also face the tactical challenge of creating an impression of themselves, a *brand image,* within the minds of potential customers. The smaller the Locust business's product or service, the less likely the customer is to invest time and energy in the pre-purchase process. In this case, a brand image can be created by consistency in both advertising and new product innovations. For Locust businesses that sell larger products or services, *reputation* must be made part of the brand image.

Black Widow businesses that wish to remain in their current situation must strive to deepen the ties between themselves and their customers. The customer is inevitably cost oriented, wanting more for less. Left unchecked, the Black Widow business's pricing and profitability will continue to fall. To maintain stability on this slippery slope, the Black Widow business must use its knowledge of the customer to endlessly *reengineer its value proposition.* By bundling multiple problem solutions into a single value proposition, the Black Widow business has the potential to offer a higher-margin total solution that its customer will find compelling.

Business Model Balancing

Let X represent a non-Chicken business and C a Chicken business. Business model balancing describes the strategies a company uses to create a corporate customer pool that contains at least one {C <->X} duo—that is, a combination of two business models that share customers. In theory, the simplest and most effective means of achieving this objective is to look for a problem to manage for existing customers.

Care must be taken, though, to ensure that the two businesses don't work at cross-purposes to each other's tactical challenges. A Pig business that is expert in sophisticated and complex skill areas may find its reputation undermined if it creates a Chicken business that manages a mundane client concern. A Black Widow business may find that its efforts to build a {C <-> X} duo spark customer concern regarding potential distractions and decreased future performance. In these and other situations, adding a Chicken business that *doesn't* share the current customers—creating a {C, X} duo—may be the preferable path to follow.

Model balancing can involve more than one step, and may thus take years to accomplish. The company that saw virtue in creating a {C, X} combination, for example, may at some later point add a new X that shares customers with the "C" model. In other words

- {X} (the starting non-Chicken business);
- {X, C} (adding a Chicken business that does not share customers);
- {X, C <-> X} (adding a new X that shares customers with C).

Alternatively, a company may create the {C <-> X} duo by adding a new non-Chicken business that has the potential to add a shared Chicken at a later date. In this case, the company that begins with X, non-Chicken business, might proceed as follows:

- {X} (the starting business);
- {X, X} (the addition of a new non-Chicken business); and then
- {X, C <-> X}, (adding a Chicken business that shares customers with the new non-Chicken).

Model balancing can also proceed in the opposite direction. The corporate customer pool can be used to assess which pieces of the portfolio "fit" and which should be considered for divestiture. This course would proceed as follows:

- *Map the corporate customer pool.* For example, a corporation may consist of five business models: X_1, X_2, X_3, C_1, and C_2.
- *Identify the combinations.* This company might have the mix {C_1 <-> X_1}, {X_2}, {C_2}, or {X_3}.
- *Evaluate linked and non-linked items.* Each piece must be evaluated. The linked pair {C_1 <-> X_1} would seem likely to be worth keeping, but nothing is cast in stone. Management might instead see a more attractive future if it finds a way to join, say, C_2 and X_2. It's possible all other units, including the {C_1 <-> X_1} combination, might be divested.

SUMMARY

While I have used C&P in my consulting work since the late 1990s, it wasn't until 2002 that I started using the framework in my classroom. Shortly thereafter one of my students asked whether I'd ever encountered a company that didn't "fit" the C&P framework.

I answered then as I do now: while the kind of two-by-two matrices I've used in this book to categorize the business world will inevitably have its limitations, the framework is universal. All businesses employ C&P because all business must define themselves in terms of the customers they serve, the solutions they offer their customers, and the revenues their solutions generate.

Thus the ideas in this chapter are not new. Virtually every one of the hundreds of executives I've known and worked with approach their businesses and their strategy development activities from the starting point of winning customers. To that extent, the methods I've described in this chapter do not belong to me; they belong to these business practitioners.

I would further assert that the ideas in this chapter are likely to prove more enduring than any strategic recommendations you've implemented in the past. I've seen executives struggle to graft new concepts or strategic frameworks onto their businesses, only to abandon them in frustration. (If I've just described your experience, I submit that the cause of past failure may have been that the ideas you tried to implement were not based on the assumption that your business must win customers to be successful.)

You won't have to strain to implement C&P. In fact, the ideas in this chapter, and indeed this entire book, should be familiar. Your business and the practices you've been trying to follow have both been described in these pages. The most difficult aspect of implementing C&P may be "unlearning" old ways of describing strategies and adopting the terms I've used to construct the framework.

The first step, analyzing your own business, will probably be the hardest one to accomplish. You may find it easier to analyze other businesses than to analyze your own. Unlike your own business, no internal politics and emotional investments need to be overcome when analyzing somebody else's business. Once you become familiar with the terms and the way they interconnect, you'll be amazed how easily you can spot the business model types outside your own business. Using the outside world as a laboratory will allow you to become adept with the framework, and you'll soon find it easy to assess your own enterprise and develop strategies to manage the customer pools you own or are contemplating.

If I've done my job, "Hold onto your customers" and "Find the Chicken" are mantras you now embrace. No doubt you've long recognized the underlying value of each, but I hope I've helped you understand more fully *why* these axioms have value. This chapter has shown how both of them can drive your future strategic journeys.

May your path be profitable.

Further Reading

INTRODUCTION

To explore the contrasting approaches to strategy, I recommend a trio of articles: Henry Mintzberg's "Five Ps for Strategy" (*California Management Review,* 1987), Michael Porter's "How Competitive Forces Shape Strategy" (*Harvard Business Review,* 1979), and Jay Barney's "Firm Resources and Competitive Strategy" (*Journal of Management,* 1991).

I strongly recommend *Strategy: A View from the Top,* by Cornelis de Kluyver and John Pearce (Pearson Prentice Hall, 2006) as a basic strategy primer. This book provides an executive overview of a wide range of topics, and its footnotes point you forward if you want to explore a topic in greater depth. My executive MBA students have warmly embraced previous editions of this volume.

Thomas Kuhn's *The Structure of Scientific Revolutions* (University of Chicago Press, 1969) is the most profound book on paradigms ever written. The book is also accessible and enjoyable to read.

The chapter references include Joan Magretta's "Why Business Models Matter" (*Harvard Business Review,* 2002) and George Yip's "Using Strategy to Change Your Business Model" (*Business Strategy Review,* 2004). The business model article I like best, though, isn't even an article about business models. It's "Are You Sure You Have A Strategy?" by Donald Hambrick and James Fredrickson (*Academy of Management Executives,* 2001). To my mind, the authors describe strategy in business model terms.

CHAPTER 1

The main research documents I used throughout this book were the annual 10K filings each cited company submitted to the Securities and Exchange Commission. The Boots and Coots story was drawn from that company's 1997 through 2005 (inclusive) 10K filings. You can obtain each of these filings—and, in fact, the data I used for every cited company—by going to the SEC website (www.sec.gov). Here's a search procedure you can follow:

1. On the SEC home page, look for the hyperlink to "Search for Company Filings."
2. On the next web page that opens, look for the link "Companies and Other Filers."
3. On this next page, enter either the company name or the stock symbol to conduct the search.

The completed search will include all company filings from all dates. You can eliminate forms you're not interested in seeing by entering "10-K" into the "Form Type" option. If this produces a list that doesn't cover all the years you want, eliminate the hyphen and try again. (Boots and Coots' initially filed 10Ks under the small business designation 10KSB and 10KSB40. They've filed 10K forms from 1999 to the present.)

CHAPTER 2

The intellectual foundation of this book's approach to business models is Derek Abell's *Defining the Business* (Prentice Hall, 1980).

CHAPTER 3

The business strategy classic is Michael Porter's *Competitive Strategy* (The Free Press, 1980). For its coverage of a wide range of basic business strategy themes and tools, I also recommend Bruce D. Henderson's *The Logic of Business Strategy* (Ballinger, 1984).

Competitive advantage has undergone significant evolution. Michael Porter's aforementioned *Competitive Strategy* identifies two types of competitive advantage: differentiation and cost advantage. His second book, *Competitive Advantage* (The Free Press, 1985), extended the thesis of his 1980 book. In *Competitive Advantage,* the author links activities performed within the company to external, competitive advantages.

"The Core Competence of the Corporation" by C. K. Prahalad and Gary Hamel (*Harvard Business Review,* 1990) takes this viewpoint one step further. This is generally considered the first significant article in what became the RBV of strategy. The RBV of competitive advantage represents the prevailing, "paradigmatic" view.

My favorite RBV exposition is D. J. Collis and C. A. Montgomery's article "Competing on Resources: Strategy in the 1990s" (*Harvard Business Review,* 1995) I also highly recommend two relatively obscure articles: Kevin Coyne's "Sustainable Competitive Advantage— What It Is, What It Isn't" (*Business Horizons,* 1986) and Mansour

Javidan's "Core Competence: What Does It Mean in Practice?" (*Long Range Planning*, 1998). Both articles exhibit a practical, applied orientation to what is largely an academic theme.

A terrific explanation of the way economics-oriented strategists see competitive advantage is found in an article by Pankaj Ghemawat and Jan Rivkin, "Creating Competitive Advantage." This is a Harvard Business School publication, #798062. You can find it at www.hbsp.harvard.edu. This article is well worth whatever effort is required to locate it.

CHAPTER 4

Corporate strategy is another of the strategy domains that has evolved significantly. Michael Porter's "From Competitive Advantage to Corporate Strategy" (*Harvard Business Review*, 1987) describes "classic" corporate strategy. D.J. Collis and C.A. Montgomery's "Creating Corporate Advantage" (*Harvard Business Review*, 1998) describes the contemporary view of corporate strategy-one rooted in the RBV of the company. An article written by Andrew Campbell, Michael Goold, and Marcus Alexander, "Corporate Strategy: The Quest for Parenting Advantage" (*Harvard Business Review*, 1995), takes this contemporary view one step farther.

Richard P. Rumelt's work remains a powerful influence in the corporate strategy domain. His *Strategy, Structure, and Economic Performance* (Harvard University Press, 1974) is a classic.

Perceiving a company's mix of business units as a portfolio and mapping these entities on a single matrix were two themes most famously introduced by the Boston Consulting Group matrix (see B. Hedley's article, "Strategy and the Business Portfolio," (*Long Range Planning*, 1977).

Index

CPSIA information can be obtained at www.ICGtesting.com
Printed in the USA
BVOW04s1853241114

376543BV00001B/3/P